D1598223

No Different than You

No Different than You

Shevi's Story

Yehudis Bogatz

English Edition

Translated by Ruth Lewis
Revised and Edited by Dvora Kiel

TARGUM/FELDHEIM

First published 2001
Copyright © 2001 by Yehudis Bogatz
ISBN 1-56871-281-2

Published by:
TARGUM PRESS, INC.
22700 W. Eleven Mile Rd.
Southfield, MI 48034
E-mail: targum@netvision.net.il
Fax toll free: 888-298-9992
www.targum.com

Distributed by:
FELDHEIM PUBLISHERS
202 Airport Executive Park
Nanuet, NY 10954

Printed in Israel
Cover design: D. Liff

Contents

INSTEAD OF AN
INTRODUCTION...

Dear Shevi,

I sit here looking at the many pages we wrote together. It was you who wrote them — with your life; I have merely rendered them in print.

I am reminded of the parashios *Acharei Mos, Kedoshim,* and *Emor.* Usually, it's only after an individual dies (*acharei mos*) that people tend to say (*emor*) how holy (*kadosh*) he was. You, Shevi, were clearly holy — in every sense of the word — your entire life!

We wrote this book together; you read most of the chapters. Together we grappled with the question of whether to publish it or not; together we decided that we would rather hear people say, "Hey, look! It's the lady from the book," when they gawked and goggled at you, rather than, "Hey, look at the midget!"

We deliberated late into the night whether or not to lay bare the story of your life. I still remember the night you finally told me, "Yehudis, even if only one person changes his or her attitude toward me or toward anybody else, I feel that accomplishment will outweigh the loss of my privacy. I feel that it will be worth the pain of disclosing all my thoughts and feelings."

Your words were like a ray of light penetrating the darkness. They warmed me more than the sun and banished the chill of years of derision that froze our hearts.

Shevi, I promised to finish your book this year, even though I had no idea how to end it — or so I thought. As always, you took care of everything. With your passing, you yourself wrote the final chapter. Indeed, the Hebrew edition of this book appeared in print exactly thirty days later, on the *sheloshim*.

Shevi, as I wrote this book and saw it through the various stages of publication, I was aware of a special gift of illumination from on High. I was ever aware of the important task I had undertaken. In your enduring wisdom, you knew that it was time for the public to be awakened, for every individual to conduct his own moral stocktaking and decide: "What sort of person am I? Am I sensitive and caring, like those who were true friends to Shevi all the way, who knew how to respect, appreciate, and love, despite life's buffeting? Or am I indifferent and careless, like those who determine the worth of a person according to his height?"

Shevi, for you it is too late to benefit from the public awareness we hope this book will arouse. But we hope that with each pure resolution formed, with every decision reached, your soul may soar higher and be bound in the bond of eternal life.

Your sister,
Yehudis

FOREWORD

*N*o *Different than You* is the story of Batsheva Wittow, "Shevi," of blessed memory, whose being was infused with great joy amid much suffering and pain. Shevi loved sunlit days, Shabbos evening strolls, sitting with good friends outdoors, and holding long telephone conversations with them at home. Her soul thirsted for friendship and acceptance. Despite her travail, Shevi always clasped joy to her heart. She knew how to focus on the good and ignore the pain.

Shevi was blessed with some excellent teachers — some more caring, some less so. There were those who understood, and those who wanted to understand, but did not know how.

I remember the wonderful loving-kindness of Mrs. Tzippora Heisler, the principal of Shevi's elementary school, who always, always understood, whose ears were ever attuned to each murmur of distress.

Another very fine teacher, who wants to remain nameless, faithfully visited Shevi in the hospital and was a great support to her when she was in pain. Shevi sang her praises until the end.

During Shevi's seminary years, her principal, Rabbi Yeshaya Lieberman, *shlita*, and his wife made her feel worthwhile and respected at all times and in all circumstances. Shevi never forgot the transatlantic telephone calls she received from them. She also cherished the letter she received in Boston from the entire school staff.

Shevi especially valued the outstanding devotion and selfless dedication of Mrs. Mintzer.

In high school she had one homeroom teacher who taught all the students how to treat others with understanding and respect by her own example, and who guided her young charges along the true path of "giving."

With this book, I want to awaken the public to awareness of those who suffer pain. I don't want to accuse; I don't want to preach. I just want people to *think* before they speak, or act, or draw conclusions.

I want people to heed the wordless, anguished cry, the silent scream of those in torment.

And I want to thank all those good people who helped make Shevi's perilous journey through life a little easier.

This book will not encumber the reader with discussions of medical treatment, and the chronological sequence of events will be obscured in order not to injure those who lacked awareness. Some names have been changed.

We pray that the reader learn from this book the lesson of *Pirkei Avos* (2:5): "Do not say, 'When I have time, I'll study,' for you may have no time!" Fine resolutions, worthy determinations so often go unrealized. Please, let us not allow the winds of forgetfulness to sweep away the good resolutions we have taken on!

"And may Hashem wipe away the tears from every face."

(*Yeshayah* 25:8)

I cannot conclude without expressing my gratitude to:

- HaRav HaGaon Rabbi Chaim Pinchus Scheinberg, *shlita*, Rosh HaYeshivah of Yeshivas Torah Ore, who has accompanied our family with "wisdom and good counsel" at all times and in all seasons, in sorrow and in joy, and whose blessings have been a wellspring of strength for us all.

- Rebbetzin Bessie Scheinberg, *shetichyeh*, who has taken such an interest all along and whose good wishes have warmed our hearts.

- Rebbetzin Ruchoma Shain, *shetichyeh*, who was there with us during heart-stopping moments. Her wise advice, flowing from pure fear of Heaven, has contributed so much.
- My dear husband, who, with endless self-sacrifice, made it possible for me to spend Shabbosos, festivals, and nights on end with my sister. He encouraged me and helped me, often late into the night, and spurred me on to complete this book so quickly.
- My dear parents, who gave of themselves and their time with great perspicacity to bring to the surface many forgotten memories which form the basis of this account. They cared for Shevi with words of praise and gratitude to Hashem for having granted them this treasure. May they merit to see much joy from all of us, in health, happiness, and prosperity.
- My father-in-law and mother-in-law, whose help and support allowed me to spend precious time with my sister during the last Shabbosos of her life, and whose assistance enabled me to expedite the publication of this book.
- Shevi's devoted husband, Rabbi Tzvi Gura, who walked together with her along the paths of pain; who helped and encouraged her and gladdened her heart always. "In the continuation of your Torah studies, may you find solace."
- Shevi's father-in-law, who constantly supported them, even in the most difficult times.
- Shevi's mother-in-law, *a"h*, who knew how to instill in her a feeling of belonging and of dignity, who listened to her words and enjoyed her wisdom and always appreciated her true worth.
- My sister Esther, who gave wise advice and understanding support, and never stinted of her energy; she sat beside Shevi day and night, during the years of dialysis and in the terminal stages of her illness, performing acts of selflessness that in some cases others knew about, but in many other cases that were hidden. She merited bringing her son into the Covenant

of Abraham just a half hour after the passing of our sister Batsheva, *a"h.* May it be His Will that her son Menachem be a consolation and a comfort. "May Hashem reward her, and may her reward from the Creator be complete."

- My sister Tovah Leah, who always knew how to cheer Shevi with wit and humor, over the telephone, at family gatherings, and on countless other occasions. She never failed to appreciate Shevi's lofty qualities and encouraged them.

- Shevi's twin sister Basha, whose helping hand was extended from the beginning, with gentleness and with love; who suffered in her suffering and rejoiced in her joy. May the merit of her devotion stand by her.

- Our brother Moshe, who always honored Shevi. With great dedication, he saw to it that prayer and Torah study be increased in hopes of her recovery.

- Shevi's sisters-in-law, who cared for her devotedly and always made her feel that she belonged.

- The many friends who supported our family during the most difficult and painful times.

- Rabbi Binyamin Fischer, chairman of Magen L'Choleh Society, who eased our family through medical problems during the last month of Shevi's life. May Hashem grant him heavenly assistance in his work of *chesed* and may he merit to see many occasions of rejoicing.

- Mrs. Shoshana Hochwald, editor of the Hebrew version of this book, who worked long and late hours, with great dedication and always with a smile.

May Hashem reward them, and may their reward from the Creator be complete.

Yehudis Bogatz
Iyar 5758

CHAPTER ONE

A RAY OF HOPE FROM BOSTON

જ઼ જ઼

*I*t was five A.M.

The sharp ringing of the telephone pierced the stillness of our home.

My mother picked up the receiver and answered sleepily, "Hello.... What?.... Who's speaking?"

The twins, sleeping in the next room, awoke. Bashi leaned down from the upper bunk and said to Shevi, "A phone call! Who could it be?"

Shevi shushed her so they could listen.

"What?... Really?"

Then they heard Mommy crying. Bashi and Shevi stared at each other, wide-eyed, alarmed. Mommy is a very special person. She is strong-willed and always knows how to cope, no matter what. If Mommy was crying, something serious had happened.

They heard Mommy open the closet. Getting dressed? In the middle of the night?

The girls were really alarmed now.

"I can't stand it," Bashi declared. Nimbly, she climbed down from the upper bunk. The door opened, and Mommy stood there looking in.

"You're up?" she said with a smile.

"Who phoned? Mommy, tell us. What's the matter?" the twins asked in concern.

"I'll tell you if you give me a chance," Mommy laughed. "It was a long distance call from Boston..."

They stared at Mommy, hardly daring to believe their ears. They knew immediately it must be about a transplant for Shevi.

"...to let us know there's a possibility.... Now, Shevi, they emphasized that it's only a possibility, but they might have a kidney for you."

Shevi's eyes shone; she was exultant. "When will we know for sure?" she asked, ever the practical Shevi.

"They said there are two people before you on the waiting list, but we should prepare ourselves. If the kidney is not compatible for either of them, then it's yours!"

The twins threw their arms around each other, shouting, "*Halevai!* If only it comes true!"

"We have to find out right away if there's a flight to Boston. Since it's such a long way from Yerushalayim to Boston, they want us to make arrangements to leave immediately."

Bashi and Shevi put on bathrobes and followed Mommy and Abba into the kitchen.

Fortunately, our father is a travel agent, and that was a big help in getting things moving that night. Abba sat down at his desk in our kitchen (he has a corner reserved for his "home office"), and began to search through the flight schedules he keeps near the telephone. The girls watched as Abba found the Boston flight list and studied it.

Mommy hurried over to the laundry corner of the kitchen and began to prepare a load to go into the washing machine. "I have to get everything organized here before we go! I can't leave all this for Abba and Bashi to do."

Shevi waited tensely for the phone to ring again. She had been awaiting a kidney transplant for nearly a year, her medical situation growing more precarious each day.

The phone rang. Abba answered. In an unsteady voice he read from the schedule in front of him and conferred a bit longer on the phone. When he put down the receiver he turned to Shevi with moist eyes and said, "Well, Shevi, it seems the kidney is compatible for you — only for you!"

Shevi's eyes rested on the red stepstool standing next to the refrigerator.

Maybe, just maybe, she thought to herself, *I won't need the footstool anymore. Maybe, after the transplant I'll begin to grow...and be able to reach the dishrack over the sink and wash dishes...without the footstool anymore.*

"But what about Tovah Leah?" Shevi suddenly asked.

"Yes," Mommy said. She looked seriously at Abba. "We have to talk about that."

"It'll be all right," Abba reassured her.

Just then Tovah Leah herself walked into the kitchen, rubbing sleep from her eyes, but her blond hair looking neat, as usual. "Hey, what's going on? Why is everyone up at this hour?"

Strictly speaking, not "everyone" was awake. Our little brother Moishy still slept soundly in his room down the hall, I was fast asleep in my home nearby, and Esther, our eldest sister, was sleeping, too, in her apartment in another neighborhood.

Mommy turned a pitying glance on Tovah Leah.

"Mommy, what's happened? Why are you looking at me like that?" Tovah Leah asked.

"Shevi is going to America," Bashi announced, "for a transplant!"

Tovah Leah looked around in confusion. Mommy sat down and said firmly, "No arguments, now. You finish making all the arrangements today, Tovah Leah. You are not to wait for me. Go ahead with your plans, and...have a beautiful party, do you hear?"

"Without you?" Tovah Leah asked.

"Oh, yes, Tovah Leah. The *tenaim* will go on without me. You may not postpone it."

Tovah Leah was to become engaged that night. The *chasan's*

parents intended to come to our house early that evening and settle the final details.

"I will call you from Boston tonight," Mommy said firmly, "and I hope to hear the sounds of a v...very h...happy engagement party going on." Mommy stood up and hurriedly left the kitchen.

Abba called Esther at that point, but no one answered. He stood up.

"The plane takes off at 7:20 A.M. Bashi, will you come with me to my office to pick up the tickets?"

Bashi ran to get dressed. Shevi followed her into their room and started to pack some clothes for the trip. Even in her haste, she packed neatly. The house was in an uproar; everyone scurried about. Abba and Bashi dashed out the door, down the stairs, into our white station wagon, and sped off to Ben Yehudah Street. Somehow, they reached the office safely, but as no parking is allowed on that street, Abba asked Bashi to wait in the car...just in case.

Sure enough, a policeman was patrolling, and stopped next to the car.

"You're not allowed to park here," he informed her sternly and started to write a ticket.

"Yes, we know," stammered Bashi, "but...."

"But what?"

"Well, you see, my sister has to go to America for a transplant operation. And she has to catch the plane, and my father has to buy the tickets, and there's no time, and...."

Her words tumbled over each other and her heart was pounding.

Abba came running out of the building with the tickets in his hand, ignoring the police officer.

"Just a minute," the policeman bellowed. "Where do you think you're going?"

"Well, you see, it's just that my daughter isn't well...." Abba spoke quickly, in American-accented Hebrew. "She is getting a transplant, now, very urgent."

The police officer's eyes lit with understanding. He wished them well, shook Abba's hand, and watched them speed away. Fortunately, at that hour there was little traffic, and they arrived at my house in a few minutes. The plane would leave in just over an hour and it would be touch and go to make it in time.

Bashi got out of the car and ran to ring my bell. She pressed the intercom button again and again; Abba punched the car horn nervously. I slept through it all.

Abba saw an acquaintance passing by. He called the man over and begged him to please do a big favor in an emergency, go up to the seventh floor and tell his daughter, Mrs. Bogatz, to call her mother immediately — tell her they had to go to the airport as soon as possible and...thanks a lot! They drove off.

The man graciously did as Abba asked. First, he tapped politely at my door. No response. Then he banged loudly. Still no response. But he didn't give up. Meanwhile, I dimly heard something in my sleep. I wondered what it could be. Suddenly I opened my eyes, realized someone was knocking, and hurried to answer the door with not a little trepidation.

"Who is it?"

"I'm a...a messenger from your father," the voice answered. "He said to telephone right away. It's urgent. He says he has to go to the airport soon."

"All right!" I called out. "Thank you!"

I tried to think. What could be so urgent? But wait a minute! Where could I phone from? We had been living in the building only a few months and my telephone was not yet connected. I didn't know the neighbors too well. Whom could I ask?

A minute later, I was knocking nervously on my next-door neighbor's door. I excused my abrupt, early visit and received her permission to use the telephone.

My parents' phone was busy, but on the third try, it rang. "Hello?"

"Shevi, it's Yehudis. What's the matter?"

"Yehudis, I'm leaving soon for a transplant. We're going to Boston," she said tranquilly.

"You're what?" I shivered. "I don't understand...."

Shevy laughed softly and told me what had happened. "Mommy wants Motty to drive us to the airport please, because we have to be there in less than an hour, and he's a fast, safe driver. Abba is too excited to drive anyway. Here's Mommy."

Mommy quickly repeated what Shevi had told me. "So be downstairs in front of your building in twenty-five minutes, okay? Or start walking toward our building. See you...."

I put down the receiver, said a hasty "thank you!" to my neighbor, and left. My head was spinning.

My husband, Motty, wasn't home from shul yet. I thought maybe I'd better daven...no, every second counted.... I should get ready.

The minute Motty returned from shul, I started to explain, but the sound of the buzzer from downstairs interrupted me.

"They must be here already."

We signalled to them from the balcony, then raced downstairs. Where were they?

"They're probably turning around; they'll be here in a minute," Motty tried to calm me.

I stood with my hands on my waist, staring down the road. Many cars passed, but there was no sign of the white car.

"They aren't answering," Motty called from the other side of the street. "They are probably on the way," he added quickly, when he saw my face turning white.

What if they had gone without us? Maybe they hadn't had time to wait. "I must say goodbye to Shevi," I whispered, my heart pounding.

With a loud screech of the brakes, the white car pulled up.

Abba moved over, relinquishing the driver's seat to my husband. I slid into the back seat next to Mommy and the twins.

"You'll have to drive really fast," Abba said. "The plane takes off in thirty-five minutes."

"But drive carefully," Mommy begged. "It's better to miss the plane than have an accident, God forbid."

Once we left the city limits, we flew along the highway. We sat in petrified silence, terrified that they would miss the plane. Abba filled in the tickets and explained the flight plan to Mommy.

"You have to fly from Tel Aviv to Amsterdam and change planes there for London. In London you'll have to change planes again for New York. In New York, you'll have to catch the plane for Boston...."

"The only problem is, if any of those planes is late, we'll miss our connections," Mommy said in a shaky voice.

"True," Abba said, "but the only direct flight doesn't leave until tonight. The doctor said that might be too late. If a kidney isn't transplanted within twenty-four hours, it might not be any good."

Mommy sighed. I looked at her, but her face revealed nothing. Impossible to guess what she was feeling. Only her fingers, drumming on her purse, betrayed what I already knew: Mommy did not like traveling — she was uncomfortable about flying. Born in the United States, she'd been living in Eretz Yisroel for twenty years and had only been back once for a visit. After that trip, I remembered, she had mentioned how hard the trip had been for her and said she simply couldn't understand how Abba was able to return every year to visit his mother.

I recalled one evening in particular, when we were sitting together on the balcony of my parents' apartment. We'd been discussing the possibility of a transplant for Shevi — what we would do if they informed us on *erev Shabbos* that a kidney was available and other hypothetical situations.

"Who'll go with me?" Shevi had suddenly asked.

"Mommy will go," said Abba, "and I'll join you a week later. I'd have a lot of things to take care of here before I could get away."

Mommy said doubtfully, "Yes, but...without you?"

We understood Mommy's misgivings.

"Are you afraid?" I'd asked.

"A little," she'd admitted shyly.

So I knew Mommy was frightened, though she wasn't showing it. I knew she wasn't even taking in what Abba was telling her.

"Write it all down in my notebook," she said, handing Abba her yellow notebook. Abba jotted it all down as the car ate up the miles. We all leaned forward in our seats, willing the car forward, forward...realizing it wouldn't help, but not knowing what else to do.

We arrived at Ben Gurion Airport with minutes to spare. We ran into the departures building; Abba went to the ticket counter, and Mommy hurried off to buy reading material for the trip, for she anticipated many hours of sitting by Shevi's bedside.

A tall, elegantly coiffed airline agent came toward us. "Where's your mother?" she demanded.

"Uh...she's buying something for the trip," I said.

"What? Go get her right away! The plane is ready to take off!" she answered.

Mommy was already on her way over, but we called out to her to hurry. She began to run toward the escalator. It was the first time I'd ever seen my poised, ladylike mother running! I will never forget it.

The airline agent and the flight manager ran alongside, urging them to hurry because the plane was waiting for them.We quickly hugged Mommy and Shevi and started to kiss them goodbye. The agent and the flight manager scolded, "There's no time for kisses. The plane is waiting!"

Nevertheless, I clung to Shevi, hugging her tight. "We'll

pray for you, Shevi," I whispered. She looked up at me with those enormous green eyes of hers full of gratitude.

Through the gates they went. Suddenly, Shevi stopped and turned around.

"Bashi," she called out, "make sure to give Shoshi carbon paper to copy my schoolwork!" The agent turned her around and pushed her onto the airport bus. She turned just her head to call back, "All right?"

"All right, Shevi," Bashi promised.

That was our Shevi — about to embark on a wearying, frantic journey, about to undergo an extremely difficult, life-threatening operation that would bring with it much all-too-familiar suffering and pain, yet she still worried about her responsibilities. She never wanted to use her illness as an excuse. She always tried to do the maximum, in spite of all the obstacles, and be like everyone else.

We drove home; Abba was now at the wheel. There was no rush. We sat in silence, all thinking the same thoughts, suffering the same anxieties. Would they get to Boston in time? Would the operation succeed? Would Shevi's body accept the new kidney, or, Heaven forbid, would it be rejected after all?

I gazed out of the window, but I didn't see the beautiful scenery passing before my eyes. My thoughts went back to those earlier days, the days when Shevi was still at the beginning of her journey....

CHAPTER TWO

IT'S TWINS!

❧ ❧

"*Mazal tov! Mazal tov!*" Savta shouted into the telephone. "Twin girls? I can hardly believe it! Oh, how I always wanted twin girls. Now my own daughter has given me twin granddaughters!"

Our grandmother turned to us in excitement with tears of joy coursing down her cheeks. "Girls, listen! You have twin sisters!"

I was five years old, my sister Esther seven. We grabbed each other and danced around, singing merrily, and Savta clapped in rhythm. Our baby sister Tovah Leah was just two, standing up in her playpen and crying, wanting to join whatever was going on.

"Tovahle," said Savta, picking her up and hugging her tight, "you have twin sisters!"

"Twin sisters?" Tovah Leah repeated with a babyish lisp. Savta twisted one of her blond curls as the tears started up again. We looked at her in alarm.

"Why are you crying, Savta?" asked Tovah Leah.

"I'm crying...for joy," she answered.

The front door opened. Abba stood in the doorway.

"Abba! Abba!" We pounced on him. He gave me and Esther a hug and picked Tovah Leah up; she wrapped her arms around his neck. He asked us if we were happy.

"Oh, boy!" I gave a jubilant shout. "Tomorrow I'm going to tell my kindergarten teacher."

"I'm going to take candy to school tomorrow," Esther announced gleefully.

"Good! Fine! You can both take candy to school." Abba smiled tiredly.

By now, the neighbors had seen the white station wagon parked out in front. They knocked on the front door one after another, and came in to wish us *mazal tov*. Everyone was thrilled for our *simchah*.

The next day Abba hung up a sign on the door: *"Mishenichnas Adar marbim b'BANOS!"* ("When the month of Adar arrives, girls increase" — a play on the traditional saying: "When Adar arrives, joy increases.")

"You were also born in the month of Adar," Abba told me. "Now I have three daughters born in Adar!"

"And when I was born," I asked hesitantly, "were you also glad?"

"Of course, my dear!" he held me tight. "Of course I was."

"How is Hannah?" Savta asked.

"She...had an operation."

"Has she recovered from the anesthesia yet?"

"Yes, but she's still a bit woozy," Abba informed her.

Finally Abba was able to get to the telephone to call his mother in the United States and break the good news to all the relatives there. So many things were going on at once: Abba talking on the telephone, Tovah Leah on Savta's lap, neighbors coming and going and leaving all sorts of cakes on the dining room table, Esther and I dipping our fingers into all the different cake frostings and licking them. The place was jumping and we felt that life was one big party.

Soon Mommy came home...without the twins. She explained to us in her gentle voice, "They are still very small. They have to stay in an incubator for a few days until they get stronger." She sat at the big kitchen table, sipping steaming coffee from a mug and looking a bit pale.

"What do you think we should name the twins?" she asked us. "How do you like Basha and Batsheva — Bashi and Shevi? That sounds good, doesn't it?"

We were very pleased with the nicknames.

Two days more, and the twins were home in their crib, lying side by side. We were amazed at how alike they were.

A month passed. Mommy seemed tense. I tried to figure it out. Wasn't I being a good girl? Had I done something wrong? Then I overheard Mommy talking to Savta. "I'm worried. The doctors think Shevi has...a problem."

A problem? I tried to hear what Mommy was explaining to Savta, but she lowered her voice. I strained to hear, but as I lay in bed listening, sleep overcame me. The next morning I hurried to the twins' crib and studied them, looking from Shevi to Bashi, from Bashi to Shevi. I didn't see any problem.

When I came home from kindergarten at noon, I tried again to discover Shevi's problem. All that day, I tried to listen in on Mommy's conversations. I knew it wasn't nice to listen, but I was really afraid inside. And I could see Abba's worried face....

I concentrated on my crayon box. Twenty-four colors! It was always so hard to choose. Suddenly I tuned in to Mommy's conversation with Savta.

"Mom," Mommy said in a trembling voice, "I'm afraid." Savta looked at her apprehensively. I held the blue crayon tightly, almost breaking it, and listened intently.

"I was at the hospital this morning with Shevi. The doctors took an X-ray." Mommy fell silent.

"And what do the doctors say?" questioned Savta quietly.

"They say Shevi has a problem with her kidneys. They're not functioning and she's going to need extensive treatment. Kidneys are supposed to filter the blood, to clean out impurities. If the kidneys don't function, then...then there are many things she won't be allowed to eat, and...." Silence. Savta squeezed Mommy's hand.

"Oh, Mom!" Tears rolled down Mommy's cheeks. "If I could only go back to the time when I could bury my head in your lap, and all the bad dreams would go away! If only you could tell me now, '*Mein tochter'l*, everything will be all right!' But I'm afraid Shevi's condition is...more serious than we thought. She'll have to go through who knows how many operations. Who knows if she can...survive them?"

At five years old, I really didn't understand too well what I'd heard. But I knew something was drastically wrong. I went into their room and stood next to the crib looking down at the twins. Shevi and Bashi were cooing to each other in their own language. I wondered what they were saying to each other.

"Oh, Shevi," I sighed, stroking her cheek lovingly. This tiny baby had no idea of what lay ahead of her, what battles she would have to fight in this world. Not one of us could foresee what a hard life she would have.

CHAPTER THREE

RIDE A WOODEN PONY

ﻪ ﻪ

*T*he years flew by; the twins were three years old. Bashi ran around on chubby little legs, but Shevi lay on her back all day, her large green eyes studying the ceiling in speculation and perplexity.

Bashi always seemed to be occupied with her friend who lived on the floor above us. "I'll be back soon," she'd call out to Shevi, and disappear. In twenty minutes or less, she'd be back with flushed cheeks and a candy in her hand. "Here," she'd say happily to Shevi, "Ricki's mommy gave me two!"

Shevi never forgot to thank her twin.

As young as she was, Bashi had already assumed responsibility for Shevi. Even then, she seemed to feel a deep need to look after Shevi, and was troubled by the many things her sister couldn't enjoy. Little did she imagine that in the future she would have to defend Shevi from the probing stares and crude, thoughtless comments of others.

One afternoon, as I was looking at Shevi lying in bed, I announced that I would take her for a walk. Mommy's face lit up. "But will you be able to manage, Yehudis?" she asked me.

"Oh, yes!" I answered.

Mommy dressed Shevi in a pale pink dress embroidered with a pair of white doves. I looked for matching socks. There were many pairs of socks in the drawer, a different pair to match each of Shevi's outfits. Mommy, you see, was always most particular about how Shevi was dressed.

I took out a pair of white socks with embroidered pink doves. While Mommy gently eased them onto Shevi's spindly legs, I removed a pair of dove-shaped barrettes from our barrette box. Mommy combed Shevi's skimpy hair and fastened on the barrettes. Dressing Shevi would sometimes take half an hour because she had to be handled very gently so she wouldn't be hurt.

When she was ready, Mommy seated her in her stroller and I, her eight-year-old sister, went downstairs with her to take her for a walk.

"Doesn't the child eat?"

"Why is she so skinny?"

Each passerby felt compelled to comment on Shevi's appearance. I can remember a stout lady wearing a green dress who stopped me.

"Tell your mother to feed the child cereal," she ordered.

As I walked on, I wondered if Shevi realized she was being stared at. Her wide-open, questioning eyes told me she did, though she said nothing.

I met my friend and classmate Yedida. "Are you embarrassed?" she asked me. "I mean...that the teacher might see...your sister?"

"Of course I'm not embarrassed," I explained. "I'm proud of Shevi!" I continued walking.

Then I met Sarale, another classmate. "The principal's over there," she warned.

"So?" I asked.

"Well, uh...she...she'll see your sister!"

I swept by her haughtily and headed directly over to where the principal of our school was standing. But suddenly Shevi cried out, "I want to go home!" I saw tears in her eyes.

I knew Shevi was uncomfortable and all the commiserating looks were upsetting her. Even though she was so young, she just couldn't bear it.

"Shevi, I just want to say hello to the principal. I want her to meet you, sweetheart," I explained as I bent over to kiss her.

"Aren't you embarrassed?" she asked, looking up at me with those huge, green, black-lashed eyes.

"Don't be silly," I answered with another kiss. "I love you!"

"Hello," I said to the principal.

"Hello, Yehudis," she said, smiling, and started to turn away.

"This is my sister Shevi," I announced importantly, stroking Shevi's cheek.

"Oh, isn't she sweet?" the principal exclaimed with a friendly smile. "You're a real mommy's helper, aren't you?"

"Yes, ma'am," I answered shyly, and we walked away.

We stopped then and I sat down on a bench. I told Shevi how much the principal had enjoyed meeting her. She rested those enormous eyes on me, and was silent.

"I don't want to be picked up," Shevi told Abba one morning. Even then, she wanted to be like everybody else; even then, she didn't want to be different. Wise Shevi — she understood so much!

Abba told us he and Mommy were going out for a little while. Esther, our big sister, was to be in charge.

My friend Tzippy came to play with me and we were soon engrossed in an interesting game. Bashi disappeared as usual, in search of her friend Ricki. Esther sat chattering with her friend Devora on the sofa. Shevi was left alone in her room, in her bed, staring into space.

Where is everyone? she wondered, feeling bereft. She began to cry softly. Her doll had fallen to the floor and she couldn't reach it.

"Bashi!" she called to her twin.

Bashi was at Ricki's house.

"Esther!"

Esther didn't hear her.

"Yehudis!" she called tearfully. "Yehudis...." I was playing a game.

When Mommy and Abba finally returned, Shevi was lying

in bed weeping with rage and frustration.

"What happened?" Mommy asked in amazement. She picked Shevi up tenderly and hugged her.

"How long has she been crying?" Abba asked sternly.

"Uh...we don't know," we stammered.

"I called you, and no one answered," Shevi reproached us.

We all lowered our eyes, ashamed to look at Shevi, so thin and frail.

Abba looked thoughtfully at Shevi and whispered a few words to Mommy.

"Shevi, listen to me!" Mommy said. "Soon you won't have to depend so much on others. We've solved the problem!"

"Will Shevi be able to walk?" asked Bashi.

Shevi looked at Bashi lovingly as if to say: *Bashi, you always know what I'm thinking!*

"Let's hope so," Abba answered with a smile. "But for now, we mean something else. We have a surprise for Shevi! But you'll have to be patient; it won't arrive for two weeks."

We could hardly wait to see what Shevi's surprise would be. The two weeks seemed to crawl by. Finally Abba showed us the receipt from the post office. The surprise had arrived and he would pick it up the next day.

The morning of that special day dawned bright and clear, and a smiling sun beamed down on Shevi's slight figure lying in her bed. Five-year-old Tovah Leah asked, every ten minutes, "Where's the surprise?"

The hours crept by and we sat around making wild guesses, waiting for Abba to come home. Whatever could it be...something that would help Shevi to be like everyone?

I studied my twin sisters, whose features were so alike: the same color eyes, the same adorable upturned nose, the same mouth. Only...only one of them was so very tiny, so very thin. Bashi had such rosy cheeks and Shevi had such pale, sunken ones. I imagined how wonderful it would be if Shevi were well.

Why, they'd be as alike as two peas in a pod, they'd go marching down the street hand in hand....

Abba's voice interrupted my flight of fancy. "Girls, where are you?"

"Here," we cried out in chorus from the twins' bedroom.

In strode Abba, carrying a fairly large, gift-wrapped box with a great purple bow, with Mommy following behind. They presented the box to Shevi with a flourish. Shevi stared at it in wonder...the box was bigger than she. We read on the return address that it came from Grandma Wittow in Denver, Colorado. It was a present from Grandma.

"Open it," Mommy urged her. Shevi tried, but her little hands couldn't tear open the wrapping paper. She turned to Bashi. "Help me."

Bashi darted over and in a flash ripped off the wrapping paper. Shevi watched her enviously, while the rest of us watched Shevi with great excitement and anticipation. Abba opened the box and removed from it...a wooden pony!

We all gasped. It was a wooden pony on wheels, painted a cheerful yellow, dappled with brown, adorned with a jaunty, polka-dotted red bow tie. We all exclaimed out loud, but Shevi was, as usual, quiet. Only her huge eyes revealed her delight — mixed with puzzlement. How would a wooden pony help her walk? How could it make her feel like everyone else?

"There, now," said Abba, smiling at Shevi kindly, and he picked her up and seated her on the pony. "Now you can ride wherever you want to go, on horseback!"

Shevi tried to ride the pony, but she couldn't manage it. The sparkle in her eyes dimmed a little.

"Try again," Mommy encouraged, smiling at her warmly.

Shevi tried again, with no success; the pony didn't budge.

"I can do it," Bashi shouted.

"Not now, Bashi — Shevi is trying. Don't disturb her," Esther whispered.

Finally Tovah Leah could restrain herself no longer and gave the pony a shove. "Look, Shevi, you're riding. What fun!" she said.

Everyone clapped their hands enthusiastically and the merry sparkle returned to Shevi's eyes.

"That's how you learn," Tovah Leah explained importantly. "Little by little." We all smiled in agreement and left the room, having decided that we'd let Shevi learn to ride the hobbyhorse by herself.

Shevi labored hard for days to learn to ride her wooden pony, a task that other, younger children performed with ease. We watched her efforts; we tried to encourage her. Shevi would look at us with those beautiful eyes, large and determined, expressing her strong will to succeed, and she'd push and push.

"Why can't she make it go?" I asked Mommy quietly.

"Why is everything so hard for her?" said Esther ruefully. Mommy patted our cheeks.

"Girls, she's just not well."

Abba and Mommy were naturally distressed that the wonderful gift from Grandma had not solved Shevi's problem. However, at just about that time Abba received a phone call from a relative of his in the United States inquiring about the family and asking particularly about Shevi. Without thinking twice, Abba asked him if he would start putting on tefillin every day — for Shevi. Even if he only were to do it for a few months, Abba had a feeling that it would help. Well, the relative agreed to do it. We don't know how long he continued putting on tefillin every day for Shevi's sake, but one afternoon, about two weeks later, Shevi surprised us.

"Mommy, come here!" she called from the bedroom.

Mommy rushed into the bedroom, thinking Shevi must have hurt herself. To her astonishment, Shevi was riding the pony back and forth in the room.

"Wonderful, Shevi! That's wonderful!" Mommy cried out,

beside herself with joy. We all crowded around to see the won-drous sight: Shevi riding her pony, her eyes shining, Mommy applauding through her tears.

Soon Shevi was riding all about the house. Shevi, who had until then lain on her back with nothing to do, was busy all the time now. "Please put this towel in the laundry hamper, Shevi." "Go out on the porch and tell Bashi to come upstairs now." Shevi would gallop off at top speed to complete her many new tasks.

I remember how happy Mommy and Abba looked during those days. They would continually pause and watch how Shevi was beginning to enjoy life.

"Mommy, I want to go to nursery school, too," Shevi begged one morning at breakfast. It wasn't the first time Shevi had asked. In fact, even when she was still confined to her crib, helpless, she had pleaded to be allowed to go to school.

"With Hashem's help," Mommy always said, "you'll also go to nursery school some day. Maybe next year...."

That morning, however, as Mommy was about to answer as usual, "Maybe...soon...," Abba interrupted her. "Maybe it is pos-sible? Why don't you go down and speak to Ahuva, the nursery school teacher?"

The nursery school was situated in an apartment on the lowest floor of our building, and we even had an elevator in the building. Nevertheless, Mommy was shocked at the thought.

"Well, why not?" Abba asked. "Look how well she rides her pony. The teacher won't have to pick her up and move her from place to place." As usual, Abba was urging Mommy to do some-thing, difficult though it might be, to actively help Shevi progress.

At lunch, we learned that the nursery school teacher had told Mommy she was willing to let Shevi come to school and see how it would go. She wasn't willing to make any promises at that point; the class was large and she would not be able to give Shevi any special attention.

"We'll send her," Abba decided. We sat around the table and shared Shevi's bliss.

"Well!" Mommy declared. "This calls for a celebration! I'm taking the ice-cream cake out of the freezer, even though I made it for Shabbos." She sliced the cake and served each of us a piece on a gold-rimmed, porcelain plate. We looked happily at the cake and at Shevi...I don't know which made us happier!

Bashi hugged Shevi, exclaiming, "We'll be together, Shevi. I can't wait!" Abba snapped a picture of the excited twins.

The next morning, with birdsong in the air, we all awakened earlier than usual. Bashi tried excitedly to give Shevi all kinds of advice about a day in nursery school. I was too tired to say a word; I hadn't slept a wink from happiness...and worry. How would the other children behave toward Shevi? Would they be nice to her?

Finally, the twins were dressed and ready. Mommy took them downstairs to the nursery school. The teacher was standing at the door, talking to one of the mothers, but she turned to give the twins a big smile.

"Hello, Bashi and Shevi."

The other mother turned to stare at Shevi, who was sitting on her pony. "Is she in this nursery?" she asked loudly.

"Yes, she is," answered the teacher.

"Why is she sitting on a hobbyhorse? And how can you pay attention to all the other girls if you have to watch out for her? I don't want you taking care of this child at my daughter's expense!"

Shevi's smile froze. Mommy was a little shaken. "My daughter doesn't require special attention," she said in her best, American-accented Hebrew. "She is a very intelligent child."

"Mommy," whispered Shevi, tugging at Mommy's skirt, "let's go home."

Mommy smoothed Shevi's hair, took her hand, and walked with her and Bashi into the apartment. The other little girls formed a circle around Shevi and Bashi.

"This is my twin sister!" Bashi proclaimed proudly.

"You are both wearing the same dress," a redheaded little girl pointed out.

All the children studied Bashi and Shevi. The twins were wearing matching yellow dresses splashed with multicolored balloons, yellow socks with the same design, and barrettes shaped like little balloons.

"You look just like each other!" said a curly-haired tot.

"That's because we're twins," Bashi explained importantly.

"So why didn't you come to nursery before?" another girl asked Shevi.

"You'll sit next to me," a very tall young lady ordered Shevi.

"No, you'll sit next to me," argued a pony-tailed miss.

Shevi smiled up at Mommy and said, "Bye, Mommy. You can go home now."

As Mommy left the room, she heard a small voice ask, "How come you're sitting on a pony?"

Mommy stopped short. She waited to hear Shevi's answer.

"Because I can't walk," Shevi explained in her thin voice.

"Why not?" they chorused.

Shevi never lost her composure for a moment. "I have an illness," she explained confidently. "My kidneys don't work...."

"But you have such a nice pony!" they replied, not understanding a word of her explanation.

Shevi gave them a friendly smile and Bashi stayed beside her to guard her from harm. Mommy stopped at the door and thanked the teacher.

"Don't worry," the teacher said soothingly. As she left the nursery school, Mommy heard the teacher leading the girls in greeting: "*Bruchah haba'ah*, Shevi. Welcome to nursery."

"I'm happy to be with you," replied Shevi in a clear, though weak voice.

CHAPTER FOUR

A MAN OF IDEAS

ॐ ॐ

*I*t was just before Purim. The twins were four years old and the wooden pony had become an inseparable part of Shevi's life and ours. Abba was concerned about how Shevi would manage to participate in our usual Purim activities. He always paid great attention to detail, and he planned ahead in just about every venture to eliminate obstacles, especially where Shevi was concerned. He had the most original ideas.

Since Abba is a travel agent, he likes to distribute *mishloach manos* packages to the various travel agencies in the city every year. We all accompanied him dressed up in costumes, and it was great fun. When the twins were infants, it hadn't been a problem. Now Abba realized it might be distressing for Shevi to be carried around like a baby or a *mishloach manos* package!

The wooden pony had certainly contributed greatly to Shevi's self-assurance. However, in town, walking among the crowds, going in and out of buildings, it would undoubtedly be difficult for her to keep up with us. If we pushed her along it would make her feel helpless, someone to be pitied. Shevi always tried to overcome obstacles by herself, on her own; she was determined to be self-reliant.

"Girls, I've got an idea!" Abba's eyes twinkled. We gathered around to listen.

"Shevi will dress up as Mordechai," Abba grinned at Shevi, "and she'll sit on the wooden horse just as Mordechai HaYehudi should!"

Shevi beamed. The horse would be a natural part of her costume. We were all delighted with his idea.

"Bashi, you'll be Haman and pull the pony along, just as Haman had to lead Mordechai's horse. And the pony will wear a sign around its neck: 'Thus shall be done to the man whose honor the king desires!' "

Bashi looked down in disappointment. Though she was only four years old, she knew she didn't want to dress up as evil Haman. We realized her disappointment immediately and were stumped. How could we explain to her how valuable her role would be? A few moments passed in silence.

Then Bashi raised her eyes, looked around at us, gave Shevi a big hug, and said in a clear, firm voice: "It will be great! Thus shall I do to the girl whose honor I desire!"

The silence continued, but it was no longer an awkward one: it was replete with emotion and happiness. Abba and Mommy's eyes were moist with pride.

Even at four, Bashi felt she must march alongside Shevi to help her overcome the many obstacles in her path. She had no idea, of course, that the role she took upon herself would be one of many years' duration.

Purim arrived. We all dressed up in costumes in a state of high excitement. Shevi sat upon her wooden pony like a real-life Mordechai and Bashi held the reins. The sign proclaimed: "Thus shall be done to the man whose honor the king desires," just as their teacher had explained it says in the *megillah*. As we left the building, passersby complimented Shevi and Bashi on their unusual costumes. Shevi's eyes sparkled with joy.

Abba parked the white station wagon outside the first travel agency on his list. "Let's go!" he said, handing out packages to each of us. "Each one of you will give a *mishloach manos* to a different person in the office." The packages were replicas of the packaged meals served by airlines in flight, and on each was pasted a note with a joke related to the travel business.

"Happy Purim!" Abba sang out, dancing into the office with us in tow. The employees were obviously not religious, but they greeted us with laughter and smiles.

"Look who's here!"

"Take a look at Mordechai and Haman!"

They rose from their seats and crowded around us. The boss remained seated at her desk, but beamed appreciatively at us. She reached into a drawer and pulled out a checkbook. As she presented us with a check for Purim gelt, she said musingly to Abba, "You certainly know how to overcome obstacles. You have a special talent for it. I should really send my daughter to spend a Shabbos with you. She might learn something."

After we left the office, Abba commented, "When wine goes in, secrets come out!"

Dark clouds covered the sun and it was drizzling. The world seemed gray and gloomy. Our mood was also gloomy; we were bickering with each other in the twins' room. Esther gazed out the window onto the rainy street. Mommy had left the room, having decided not to get involved in our squabbling. The twins, too, sat with nothing to do, Bashi on the rug and Shevi in her crib.

"Tovah Leah took my gold napkin!" I complained, crying and trying to pull it out of her hands. (We collected pretty, colored paper napkins at the time.) The napkin tore, naturally, and then Tovah Leah began to cry.

Disgusted with her cranky sisters, Shevi said in her calm voice, "Why are you all so angry? Why aren't you happy that you can walk?"

Bashi, who was also feeling kind of grumpy just then, retorted, "And do you think you'll always be happy when you can walk?"

Astonished at the question, Shevi looked around at all of us, and we waited to hear her reply.

"Of course!" she said, trembling with emotion. Suddenly she grasped at the bars of her crib...and then...and then...she was standing up!

"Shevi's standing up!" Esther and I cried out together.

"Shevi's standing!" Tovah Leah shouted, her eyes filling with tears.

Mommy and Abba hurried in to see what all the shouting was about. They stood together in the doorway and stared in amazement. There was Shevi, standing up in her crib, with flushed face and radiant eyes, smiling in jubilation.

Overcome with emotion, Abba just stood there.

Mommy went over to Shevi and hugged her. We all wiped the tears from our eyes.

During the next few days, Shevi took her first, faltering steps on tiny feet. People who had seen her sitting in her stroller, looking so fragile and small, had assumed she was paralyzed. Who would have believed that she would soon be able to run from room to room, that soon she would join Bashi in running upstairs to visit Ricki on the fourth floor?

CHAPTER FIVE

SHEVI REFUSES TO TALK

❧ ❧

Mommy tucked a warm blanket around Shevi, ensconced in the back seat of the car, and with Abba behind the wheel, they drove off. They were once again on their way to visit a doctor; this time he was a renowned specialist in Hadassah Hospital. Shevi was almost five years old and it was time to get an evaluation of her mental and motor development.

The specialist started by questioning Shevi to assess her intelligence level.

"How old are you?"

No answer.

"Where do you live?"

Shevi stared at him mutely.

The doctor kept on prodding, smiling reassuringly. Shevi said nothing.

The doctor asked her to draw a picture and handed her crayons and paper. Shevi complied. He asked her to stand and sit and turn around. Shevi complied without a word. He coaxed her; he made funny faces; he took off his white coat; he even got down on his hands and knees to amuse her. She remained unsmilingly silent. She performed whatever activity was asked of her, but refused to talk.

Mommy and Abba begged her to show the doctor how smart she was, to prove that she could communicate, and very intelligently at that. She seemed to be up to par in most areas, despite her diminutive size, but they couldn't get a word out of her.

After a half hour of this, the doctor entered a lengthy nota-
tion in Shevi's file and turned to my parents. "The diagnosis is
negative," he said sternly. He obviously had not been satisfied
with Shevi's performance.

"In my opinion, this child is developmentally impaired...."

"That's not true!" Mommy interrupted him, uncharacteris-
tically.

"I haven't finished." The doctor regarded her coldly.

"But there's no point in drawing conclusions from one interview, when we live with her and observe her on a daily basis,
and —"

The doctor polished his glasses with an immaculate, white
handkerchief. "That may be true. However, with all due respect,
you are biased. You undoubtedly interpret your daughter's every
movement as indicative of intelligence. Whereas, I —"

Again, Mommy interrupted. "Isn't fluent speech an indication of intelligence?" she asked.

"Oh, yes," the doctor conceded.

"Well, our daughter speaks extremely fluently," Mommy
informed him proudly. "She —"

Now the doctor interrupted Mommy. "As I have said, her
babble undoubtedly sounds like speech to you. Indeed, in a
younger child, those sounds are speech. But in a child of four
and a half...?"

Mommy looked at Abba, signaling a plea for help.

"Ah...Professor," Abba began slowly and clearly, "our
daughter does not babble. She speaks in clear and complete sen-
tences and can carry on a conversation."

The doctor grew impatient.

"See here," he said curtly. "I do not intend to argue with
you. I have examined your daughter for the better part of an
hour, with no response on her part. I have given you my professional opinion." He put down his pen in annoyance.

"Shevi, why won't you talk?" Mommy asked gently.

Shevi maintained her silence.

"I just don't understand it," Mommy said. "I know her intelligence is not impaired. I know she's a very perceptive little girl."

"The interview is over," said the specialist, raising his hands in defeat.

A heavy atmosphere of dejection pervaded the car as they drove home. Finally, Abba couldn't restrain himself any longer. He pulled over to the side of the road, stopped the car, and turned to Shevi.

"Shevi, why did you refuse to speak to the doctor?"

"He wasn't wearing a *kippah*, Abba," said Shevi nonchalantly.

An interesting postscript to this tale is as follows: Abba told a neighbor what had happened. This neighbor worked in the same department of the hospital as the specialist, and he found a way of conveying the explanation of the incident to the specialist. Abba was hoping, perhaps, for another appointment. The neighbor told us the doctor's response was "What? I should put on a *kippah* for that kid?"

When the reply got back to Abba, he mused to himself: "To go down on hands and knees, he was willing; to remove his white coat, he was willing. To put on a *kippah* — that was beyond the call of duty!"

Shevi, as young as she was, had a will of iron.

CHAPTER SIX

WHY SHOULD I CRY?

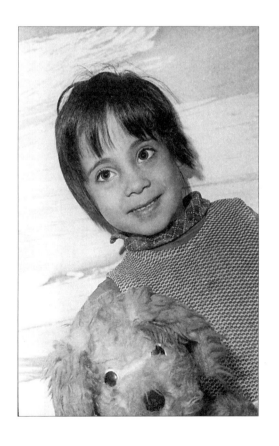

❧ ❧

"**S**hevi, didn't you tell your friends you would meet them in the playground at four o'clock? You ought to leave now."

It was only three o'clock, but Mommy was anxious. Shevi adjusted her cherry-shaped barrettes, smoothed down her cherry-patterned dress and walked out with small steps. Small? An understatement! Her steps were tiny. It was a three-minute walk to reach the playground near our house for us. All I had to do was leave the building, cross the street, and go down the hill. Shevi, with her frail legs and fragile bones, with barely the strength to walk, had to allow herself much more time. I would often offer to pick her up and carry her, but she refused.

"I'll manage," she said firmly. "I do walk slowly, but I can manage on my own, thanks. I don't have to be dependent on you."

Shevi arrived at the playground at four twenty-five, proud of her own efforts. When Shevi looked at me at times like that, her huge, green eyes glowing with wisdom beyond her years and overflowing with the joy of achievement, I felt as if I had a glimpse of a *mussar sefer*. She showed me by her example that I must always remember to rejoice in the gifts I have been granted. I can walk! I can stride along! How fortunate I am!

To arrive at school on time, Shevi used to leave about an hour ahead of time, walk slowly, and rest every few minutes. For her it was a long, long journey. The rest of us used to leave the house about forty minutes later and catch up with her midway. She'd never complain, never sigh. To all those who offered to pick her up, tiny Shevi would answer, "I'm walking, thank you — slowly, but surely."

Once Shevi was on her way to school on a dark, rainy morning, early as usual. Threatening clouds filled the sky and a strong wind was blowing, whipping the tree branches. When she was just a few feet away from the school, a sudden gust lifted her up off the ground and hurled her backward. She landed many feet behind, hitting the ground hard. She bit her lips in pain, but got to her feet without a word, shook out her skirt, and started forward again — "slowly but surely."

Moments later, another strong gust carried her backward again; this time she fell harder and landed in a puddle. She lay there in pain. A solitary tear escaped, but she dried it quickly. "Don't cry," she berated herself. "Just don't cry!"

Minutes passed; people went by, but they did not notice the very small, thin girl lying helpless in a puddle of water at the edge of the sidewalk. Shevi tried to get up. Finally, she managed to sit up, but she simply couldn't overcome the force of the wind and stand.

We came along just then. We almost didn't see her either. It was foul weather, and she was so small, sitting off to the side, shivering in the rain and wind. We were aghast. Her lips were blue with cold and she was crying.

"I can't get to school," she sobbed. Esther picked her up in strong arms.

"How long have you been lying here?" I asked.

"It feels like a long time," Shevi said, trying to hide the tears that flowed against her will, "but maybe it's only been a few minutes." Typically, it was only herself she accused — of impatience. She wasn't angry at those who had passed her by, unseeing. Anyone, anyone but Shevi would have complained how egoistic people are, how uncaring. This was a six-year-old child!

"Let's go on to school now," Shevi said, hugged close in Esther's arms.

"No, Shevi," we told her. "We're going home."

"But why?"

"Your skirt is all muddy," Bashi said. "See?" Bashi had intentionally touched on Shevi's most sensitive spot to convince her. Neither pain nor weakness were reasons to give up, but Shevi was most particular about her clothes. She took great care to keep her clothes neat and clean, and she would never consent to wearing anything with even the smallest stain.

Esther instructed Tovah Leah, Bashi, and me to go on to school. She said she would take Shevi home herself.

"We want to take Shevi home, too," we complained. "We wouldn't mind at all getting to school late for such a good reason."

Esther started to argue with us, but I took Shevi from her and headed for home. Esther had no choice. We all marched along together, an odd-looking crew: I was carrying Shevi; Esther was holding Shevi's hand; Bashi and Tovah Leah were stroking Shevi's tiny legs. Thus, under the astonished gaze of all who beheld us, our little band arrived home.

Mommy met us at the door. She was greatly alarmed and took Shevi immediately into her arms and held her close.

"What is it, sweetheart?" she asked.

We started to tell Mommy what had happened, all of us talking at once.

"I can't understand a thing," Mommy cried. "Talk one at a time!" Seeing that no one was willing to cede to anyone else, she finally said, "Shevi, you tell me."

"There was...a strong...wind, and...and...." Shevi was so overcome she couldn't say another word.

"Quick! Bring her something to drink!" Mommy told us. We all ran to help, each of us bringing her something else: Esther took her a glass of water, I, a cup of *petel* (raspberry-flavored water), and Bashi, a glass of cola. Tovah Leah thoughtfully brought a damp towel.

Mommy sponged Shevi's forehead with the towel. Then she held the raspberry drink to her lips. Shevi took two sips and pushed the cup away. Immediately Mommy tried the cola. Shevi took two sips and pushed it away. But the pallor began to leave her face, and she squeezed Mommy's hand.

"I feel...a little better...Mommy," she said faintly.

"I'm phoning the doctor," Mommy decided.

"No, no!" Shevi tried to dissuade her. "I don't need a doctor."

When the doctor heard what had happened, he told Mommy to bring Shevi right in to be examined. Mommy went into her room to get dressed.

"I also...need to...change my clothes," said Shevi weakly.

Esther smiled. "All right. Help her dress, girls."

We hurried to the bedroom to help Shevi dress. Esther stayed in the kitchen to prepare a cup of coffee for Mommy to drink before they left. I took out Shevi's blue dress; Tovah Leah found the blue stockings, and Bashi, the blue barrettes. Shevi was so weak and dizzy she could hardly stand. We were all wondering how badly she had been hurt.

"Are you ready, Shevi?" Mommy called. "And you, girls, will have to hurry back to school. You're already late!"

We smiled to ourselves. We were almost always on time. Mommy said that since we lived only five minutes away from school, there was no excuse for tardiness. This time, we had an excuse!

"Let's all go down together," I suggested, hoping Mommy wouldn't refuse.

Of course she didn't refuse. She knew we'd helped her and we deserved to "profit" from the misadventure. Mommy finished her cup of coffee while Esther ordered a cab. "He'll be here in five minutes," Esther announced.

We all rode down in the elevator.

"Just a small kiss for Shevi," we begged.

Shevi didn't like to be hugged and kissed; it made her feel like a baby. Now she was so weak, she couldn't refuse, so we all kissed her in turn. The taxi arrived and they left.

We waved goodbye as long as we could, but Tovah Leah reminded us that we had to get to school. She loved school more than any of us. Having no choice, then, we set off for school.

"What should we tell the teacher?" Bashi asked.

"We'll tell the truth!" I said bossily. "Maybe now they'll fix the railing next to the steps," I added hopefully. Mommy had asked them several times to repair the railing, realizing that it was dangerous for all the girls, but especially for Shevi. We reached the school, entered, and went separately to our class-rooms.

"Why are you late, Yehudis?"

"Well, my sister..." I started to explain.

"I asked why you were late. Don't tell me about your sister!"

I felt tears pricking under my eyelids. It wasn't fair. Why didn't she let me tell her what had happened? Everyone was looking at me. I was afraid to say another word. I decided I wouldn't say anything.

"Outside!" she ordered.

I went out into the hallway. My throat was all choked up, and as soon as the door closed, I burst into tears.

"What's the matter?" a soft voice asked.

I looked up to see the principal standing there. She didn't look angry at all. She told me to go wash my face and come back and tell her what had happened. When I returned, I felt much calmer. I was able to tell her how we had found Shevi lying in a puddle, and everything that had followed.

"Why didn't you explain all this to your teacher?" she asked kindly.

"I was trying to, but she wouldn't listen!"

"Go back to your class now. Tell your teacher I'll speak to her later."

I thanked her and entered the classroom. My teacher looked at me in askance, but allowed me to sit down.

Classes seemed unusually long that day; I was so worried about Shevi. When I arrived home at last, only Bashi was there. Mommy's coffee cup was still on the table, and of course, there was no lunch prepared.

We were so used to Mommy's sudden trips to the hospital with Shevi that we knew very well how to fend for ourselves. Just as I was preparing pizza for everyone, with yellow cheese and pitas, the telephone rang. It was Mommy, calling from the hospital.

"Mommy, how's Shevi?"

"Yehudis, is that you? Are you managing all right?"

"Yes, Mommy. I'm making pizza for everyone, don't worry. Mommy, how is Shevi?"

"Are the other girls home yet? Is everyone all right?" Mommy evidently did not want to share her anxiety with us.

"Mommy, how is Shevi? When will she come home?" I persisted.

"Well...Shevi will be...staying in the hospital for a few days. She has a slight case of shock."

"What?"

"Yehudis, finish making pizza for everyone. It would be a shame if they come home and it isn't ready."

"All right, Mommy. I'll put it in the oven now."

"Bye, Yehudis. I'll call later."

I hurried to set the table. Bashi helped me clear the leftovers from breakfast that Mommy hadn't had time to take care of. I set out the plates and cups, and even arranged the silverware properly. I felt like a little mother.

At 2:15 Tovah Leah and Esther came home.

"Did Mommy call?" Esther asked.

"Yes," I said, checking the pizzas in the oven.

"Well, what did she say?" Tovah Leah asked anxiously.

I told them that Shevi would be in the hospital for a few days and that she was suffering from shock. They sighed in commiseration. We sat down to eat, each of us thinking, *How much more must Shevi suffer? How much pain?*

At about five o'clock, Abba walked in with some news. "Esther and Yehudis may go to visit Shevi."

Bashi and Tovah Leah looked at us enviously and asked Abba why they couldn't go, too. Abba told them calmly that they would have a turn the next day.

Abba drove us to the hospital. In the children's ward, on the sixth floor, Shevi was lying in the center of a big bed, a white sheet covering most of her body, her pale face paler than usual, her arm connected to an intravenous tube. She tried to smile cheerfully at us.

"Hi, Esther. Hi, Yehudis."

"How are you, Shevi?" we asked warmly. We weren't at all disconcerted by the scene before us; we were, in fact, quite accustomed to seeing Shevi in that position.

"*Baruch Hashem,*" she answered weakly.

We helped ourselves to the candy we had brought her. Shevi looked at it longingly, but she wasn't allowed to have any. Just after we told her about everything going on at home and in school, a nurse came in and ordered us out so she could administer an injection.

When we returned, Shevi was sitting up, more or less in the same position, and she invited us to play a game of cards with her, taking a pack from the bedside cabinet. We marveled at how calm and composed she was, asking if perhaps she had not, after all, received the injection. She assured us she had received it.

"You don't act like someone who just had a painful injection," I said.

"How should I act? Should I cry or scream? Would that help? Would it change my condition? Would it..." Shevi stopped. Only her enormous, green eyes, reflecting pain and knowledge, wordlessly said the rest of the sentence. *Would crying make me healthy like everybody else?*

CHAPTER SEVEN

V.I.P. VISIT

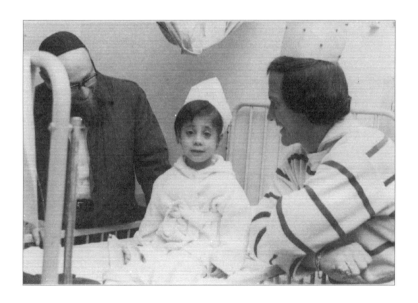

❧ ❧

Something was going on in the children's ward. Dina, the cute, charismatic nurse whom everyone loved, was on duty. Her dark, twinkling eyes and infectious laughter had endeared her to the other staff members as well as to the children. She had a joke for everyone and cheered up the most apathetic patient.

It didn't take Dina long to sense there was a mystery afoot. The other nurses were busily questioning everyone, trying to discover what was going on. Dina, in her usual forthright style, went directly over to the head of the hospital maintenance staff, Rafi, and asked point-blank what the fuss was about.

Rafi reported that he had just come from a maintenance staff meeting at which they were warned to make sure the children's ward was in tip-top shape: beds straightened, furniture in place, floors mopped clean, medical equipment in orderly array, linens in neat piles, and so on. An important visitor was due to arrive any minute to visit the children — a famous singer from the United States by the name of Pat Boone!

Dina duly reported her news to the other nurses and to the curious children. The nurses subconsciously straightened up and smoothed their uniforms. Dina looked around at the small children, all of whom were attached to various instruments. For a moment her eyes rested on Shevi, lying in bed, seemingly indifferent to the commotion going on around her.

"But why is everyone so excited?" asked Ruthie from her wheelchair.

"Well, you see," Dina explained, "this famous singer will be interviewed when he returns to America, and he'll tell everyone about this hospital."

"So what?" asked Efrat, blowing her nose.

"If he is disappointed by what he sees, many people who give money to the hospital might stop contributing, and that would be bad for us all. But if he is pleased and gives a good report,we may get lots more donations."

"Then maybe there'll be enough pajamas for all the kids?" asked Ruthie innocently. Dina laughed as she chased the children back into their beds, and went into the next room.

The telephone at the nurses' station rang. The supervisor called out, "He's here! He's on his way up to the children's ward."

The doors of the elevator opened, and there he was — a tall, slender man, accompanied by the hospital director, several photographers, and assorted assistants. Pat Boone walked from room to room, stopping to chat with each child. With someone translating for him, he graciously answered questions from the children, and asked his own questions about the machines they were hooked up to. He went from child to child, patiently, smiling at each one, and insisted on being photographed with each child.

The kids smiled for the photographer and forgot their pain for a moment. He posed with Sarale and Ruthie, Tehilla and Shmulik, Nachum and Efrat.

He arrived at Shevi's bed. He looked at six-year-old Shevi, lying so quietly. She wasn't patting her hair into place like the others; she wasn't flustered. She looked up at him with her huge green eyes so full of wisdom.

"What's your name?" the singer asked.

"Shevi," she answered softly.

Turning to the head of pediatrics who was standing at his side, the singer said quietly, "There is something very special about this child. I don't know what it is, but her face has an unusually soulful look...."

The singer looked down at Shevi, and everyone else watched them.

"I want several shots taken with her," he said decisively. "I have never seen eyes like those — so beautiful and so filled with pain and anguish. Such wise eyes, so rare...."

Moving from one side of the bed to the other, he insisted on another, and another, and another photograph. The doctors, the nurses, the other children were silent. *What was so remarkable about little Shevi?* they wondered.

The singer wished Shevi well. "Good luck to you," he said. "I know you have a difficult time ahead of you, but I know you'll pull through. You'll succeed, I'm sure of it! Be strong!"

CHAPTER EIGHT

THE SHOW IS OVER!

❧ ❧

"**D**o I look like I fell from the moon?" Shevi said scornfully. The dark-haired girl who had been staring at her blushed uncomfortably and turned away.

Shevi and I laughed. We were riding on the public bus and, as usual, some people stared rudely at Shevi. Shevi, inured to it, either returned their stare, dashed off a quip, or waved her tiny hand and said, "Hello!" The starer always turned away uncomfortably, and Shevi and I laughed together.

Nevertheless, behind the joke, her voice betrayed the anguish she felt. During the entire ride, Shevi would anticipate those stares with trepidation. When we reached our stop and descended, Shevi told me how much better it was when I was with her.

"When you're with me, I have the nerve to fire off a comment or a joke." She squeezed my hand. "When I'm by myself, it's so hard...."

We could feel the eyes upon us. I glanced at Shevi; I knew this goggling was the hardest burden she bore. I couldn't understand how people could pile more burdens on someone who already had to suffer more than her share. Couldn't they see she was aware of their gawking? Why did they all think she was deaf to their cruel comments and oblivious to their stares? Those stares pierced her like daggers and wounded her more than all the doctors' needles.

We had a few errands to do for Mommy. I suggested to

Shevi that she go into one store and I into another, and we would meet outside after we made our purchases. Shevi bit her lip and said hesitantly, "I'd...rather not. Everyone will look at me...and...."

"All right," I agreed, "we'll go in together." I knew how upset she already was. When, I wondered, would people understand that someone who is outwardly different is inwardly just like everyone else?

"Yes, may I help you?" the saleslady politely asked me.

As I started to answer, she shifted her gaze down toward Shevi and stared at her, apparently forgetting me. She stood there agape, her courteous manner gone. Naturally, other customers turned to see what spectacle had captured this "polite" saleslady's attention. Soon they all stood there, crowding around to look at Shevi.

Shevi squeezed my hand in embarrassment. I looked down at her and saw that she had turned absolutely white and her green eyes flitted from side to side in despair. I thought she was going to faint. I swallowed hard in agitation, trying to think of how we could extricate ourselves from this situation. I was afraid to say anything for fear my voice would break or I'd burst out crying. So we stood there for what seemed an eternity, but was probably less than a minute, in silence.

Did I say silence? No, there was a sound. It was a silent scream; it rose in the air above us — the cry of an anguished young girl, a scream that pleaded, "Stop staring at me! Why are you tormenting me? Don't you think I know I look different? Do you have to keep reminding me? Don't you think I feel it in every cell?"

Finally I heard myself say in a choked voice, "All right! The show...is over!"

I grabbed Shevi's hand and pulled her away, practically dragging her through the crowd of spectators.

On our way out, I heard the saleslady call after us, "Oh,

miss! What was it you wanted?"

"I wanted," I said to myself angrily, "to teach you some manners!"

As we strode along in silence, I choked back the tears. I was determined not to cry in front of Shevi. But Shevi astonished me with her tranquil comment on the whole episode. "The pain of embarrassment is an atonement for sin."

I could only nod my head in agreement.

"It's hard," she went on. "Very hard. I don't know why they do it. I try to tell myself to pay no attention, but it doesn't help." She smiled up at me bravely, and said, "Come on! Let's buy ourselves a drink!"

Once again, it was Shevi who was consoling me. I felt dwarfed beside her giant soul. Instead of my comforting her after such an unpleasant event, she was comforting me. How brave she was!

CHAPTER NINE

JUST A GLASS OF WATER

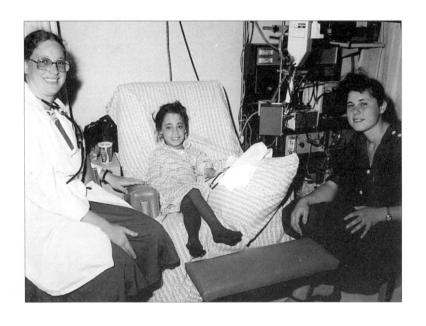

❧ ❧

S hevi was eleven years old. For some time her test results had been steadily deteriorating; the creatinine in her blood was rising at an alarming rate — a sign that the already minimally functioning kidneys had almost ceased to function.

Abba, Mommy, and Shevi were sitting in the waiting room of the clinic, waiting to hear the results of the latest blood test. Though it was in the midst of a heat wave, they were chilled with foreboding.

At last a nurse appeared and led them into the doctor's office. Abba and Mommy sat down, but Shevi remained standing. The doctor leafed through the papers in Shevi's file. The room was quiet. Abba and Mommy studied the doctor apprehensively, afraid to hear his diagnosis.

"Is it worse?" Mommy broke the silence.

"Yes."

"What can be done?" Abba asked.

"The only effective solution is...dialysis."

Abba and Mommy started to ask questions at the same time. "Dialysis?"

"What exactly does that mean?"

"For how long?"

"I'll explain," said the doctor. "Your daughter's kidneys are almost not functioning; her blood is full of impurities. You can see it in her face; her skin has taken on a yellowish tinge. That skin color is a clear indication that she's full of toxic residues — the kidneys are not filtering out the impurities from her blood as they should." The doctor inhaled and picked up a pen from the desk.

"Today, however, we have a machine, something like an artificial kidney, which can be attached to the patient to filter his blood." The doctor paused and studied Abba and Mommy.

"How...how many times does a person have to...have this treatment?" Shevi broke the silence.

"The patient has to come to the hospital three times a week to be connected to the dialysis machine."

"How...long are they connected to it?" Mommy asked.

"About four hours each time," the doctor replied. "A person's kidneys work twenty-four hours a day to filter his blood; the machine works three times a week!"

"When will we start treatment?" Abba asked nervously.

"It's not so simple," the doctor explained. "First, Shevi has to have an operation to insert a tube into her arm. The dialysis needle will be connected to that tube."

Shevi remained standing, her face expressionless. It was impossible to know how she was taking it.

"We'll talk further on your next visit," said the doctor, standing up to indicate the visit was concluded. "Meanwhile," he smiled at Shevi, "you can come and see the dialysis ward. See if it appeals to you...."

Shevi frowned, as if asking, "If it appeals to me? What nonsense!"

They left the office, each immersed in his own thoughts. Shevi was now to be a dialysis patient, yet another "honorific" for Abba and Mommy's beloved daughter. Her Book of Suffering was far from ended.

"When will I finally start dialysis?" Shevi asked impatiently. She had been awaiting her turn for weeks.

"Why are you so anxious to start?" Mommy looked at her sadly.

"Well...um...that machine looks so interesting. I've seen other children attached to it whenever I've been at the hospital, and I just want to know for myself how it feels."

"Don't worry," Mommy said sadly. "You'll get to know only too well how it feels."

Shevi never minded trying something new, and she was always curious about how other people felt or thought. She didn't stop talking about the dialysis machine; the novelty, the escape from routine seemed to attract her. She seemed to have forgotten about the operation required before she could begin treatment. Mostly, though, she was hoping the dialysis would improve her health and strengthen her.

Had she only known it would weaken her further, that it would interrupt even more the normal framework of her life, she would not have awaited it with such impatience.

Finally the day arrived. Abba and Mommy left the house early, wrapped in heavy coats against the cold. Shevi had been admitted to Shaarei Tzedek Hospital the day before to prepare for the operation. That morning a tube called a "shunt" would be inserted into her arm to facilitate what would be her regular dialysis treatments.

We children also awakened earlier than usual. Shivering in the cold apartment, we sat around the electric heater and recited *Tehillim*. We raised our eyes to Heaven and prayed, "Let everything go smoothly for Shevi...let Shevi be healthy at last!"

Esther rose from her chair and reminded us we had to get ready to go to school. As the eldest, Esther always felt she needed to be our substitute mother and she was very responsible. The twins were now in sixth grade, Tovah Leah in eighth, and Esther and I were already in high school and seminary. Moishy, our little brother, was six years old and attending cheder.

Esther made us sweet, hot cocoa, which we tried to enjoy, but found we could only think of Shevi. Nevertheless, we gulped down our breakfast and went to school.

I remember my thoughts as I rode to school that morning. I wanted to get to school and immerse myself in the lessons, to escape a bit from the tension, yet at the same time, I didn't in the least feel like studying. My mind was with Shevi. I wished I could hold her tiny hand and tell her what a heroine she was.

The day passed slowly. I told only my best friend Yedida what was going on. At recess, the class was supposed to be organizing a party to take place in a few days. I stood there in the schoolyard, handing out assignments enthusiastically, never letting on that my heart was miles away. Yedida couldn't believe how well I hid my feelings.

Back in class after recess, Yedida passed me a note: "No one could tell from looking at you that anything is going on in your family."

I wrote back: "What should I do? Sit around and mope? Unfortunately, we are used to our sister being in the hospital now and then. Don't you see? Life goes on; we can't stop it every time something happens."

She smiled and wrote back: "Yehudis, yours is a very special family!" and underlined the word "special" three times.

"Have you come to visit Shevi?" a tall, slim nurse asked me. I nodded.

"You can go right in."

Shevi was in a big room, filled with large lounge chairs in which children of different ages and backgrounds reclined. Each one was connected through tubes to a machine. In one part of the machine I could see transparent tubes full of blood. Some tubes led into the machine and others out. I was mesmerized watching the tubes. I forgot for a moment why I'd come.

"Yehudis!" I heard a gentle, familiar voice.

"Hello, Shevi," I said, in a sort of daze.

"Come here," Shevi smiled at me. "Sit down on that chair. You look scared."

Shevi looked at me with compassion. Yes, Shevi looked pityingly at me, at poor Yehudis, who was frightened by the sight of children connected to machines.

"It's not so awful." Shevi smiled again. "I'll explain how it works and you'll see there's nothing to be afraid of." I, a high school senior, stood there and listened to a medical lecture from my little sister!

"Put your hand on this tube," Shevi showed me. "See? From this tube the blood leaves my body and goes into the machine. Over here — see? — it comes out clean and goes into this tube which brings the clean blood into my body."

I felt better. The nurses smiled at Shevi's skilled explanation.

"And now, have some chocolates," offered Shevi kindly. I took a square.

"See all the candy I've been given? It pays to be on dialysis," Shevi joked, even though she was not allowed to eat most of it.

Now I laughed freely. It was always so nice to be with Shevi; she always knew the right thing to say to everyone.

I took out my small gift, wrapped in gaily-colored paper, and offered it to her. "I brought you a game."

"Oh, thank you!" Shevi rejoiced. She opened it and discovered a miniature magnetic checker game. "It's just exactly what I wanted!" Shevi always knew how to make a person feel appreciated.

"Is that really what you wanted?" I asked doubtfully.

"Oh, yes," she insisted. "I need a nice, easy game to play with whoever comes to visit me — if anyone does come to visit me in dialysis."

We chatted for two hours. A little boy wearing eyeglasses in the chair-bed next to Shevi regarded her with envy. Across from her, a rather pale, dark-haired little girl with lovely dark eyes and long lashes reclined.

"No one visits her," Shevi told me quietly. "You know, there's no family like our family!" She gave my hand a quick squeeze. "I see children sitting here for hours with nothing to do. They're sad, they're bored, they want someone to come over to them and ask how they are." Shevi took a deep breath. "I always have company: my parents, my brother, my sisters — the very best sisters in the world." She squeezed my hand again.

It was a Wednesday afternoon — not one of Shevi's treatment days. We were sitting on the balcony, on bright-cushioned lounge chairs, watching the world go by and sipping cold water from tall glasses.

"To drink a glass of water...is not so simple," Shevy pronounced suddenly.

We all looked at her.

"I said," she repeated distinctly, "that to drink a glass of water is not a simple thing."

"What on earth do you mean?" Bashi asked.

"For the fact that we can drink water, and as much as we want, we have to thank Hashem!" Shevi said. "In the dialysis ward some of the children aren't allowed to drink more than one cup of water a day. They beg and plead, 'Nurse! Nurse! Water! Water!' Yesterday a little girl in the next recliner, about eight years old, was looking at me so beseechingly that I asked her if I could do anything for her. She said, so imploringly, 'There's just one thing I want.'

" 'What do you want?' She said I wouldn't be able to help her. I told her my sisters were coming soon and they would be able to get it for her. So I asked her again what it was she wanted. 'A glass of water!' she told me.

" 'My sisters will bring you a glass of water,' I told her in astonishment.

" 'No,' she said. 'I'm not allowed....'

"I was thunderstruck. I had never heard of such a thing. I'd heard of not being allowed to eat candy, cakes, bread — but a glass of water!

" 'Yes,' the little girl told me. 'And I'm so thirsty....' "

Shevy ended her story. We were speechless.

"We don't know how lucky we are," Shevi exclaimed, with great feeling. "We can drink as much water as we want!" And she picked up the pitcher of water and poured out a glass of clear, cold water.

Again, tiny Shevi — so small, so great in spirit — was teaching all of us about the important things in life. She did not mention, of course, the fact that she herself was forbidden to eat bananas, cake, cookies, Bisli, Bamba, or any of the candies she loved so much. The fact that she had been warned against salt, even in salads, was also forgotten. The main thing was that she could drink water — as much as her heart desired. Her eyes reflected her deeply felt joy as she sipped her glass of water.

CHAPTER TEN

NO END TO PAIN

છે. છે.

Abba loves to buy books. Before every *yom tov*, he would buy us each a new book, taking Esther with him to help choose. "You can't have too many good books," he always said.

Esther's help was supposed to be a secret, though, and we all acted as if Abba had chosen the books himself.

"It's just what I wanted," I would exclaim, on seeing the title of the book. "How did you know?"

"I know your taste," he would answer, his eyes twinkling and a smile gleaming through his beard.

It was Sukkos, and each of us had received our book. We settled down in various comfortable chairs and immeditaely began to enjoy our gifts. Bashi's book was a thick one, with small lettering and no Hebrew vocalization. "What a great book," she remarked several times.

Shevi picked up her slender volume with an endearing smile. Her book had large print and all the Hebrew vowels written in.

"That's a great book, too," Bashi consoled her.

"A book for babies," Shevi said sadly. "I only hope I can finish it."

Bashi went over and gave Shevi a big hug. "With Hashem's help, Shevi, you'll also be able to read books like ours," she said softly. "And then you'll have so many new books to read, we'll be jealous of you, because we'll already have read them."

"You're right," Shevi said, trying to hide her doubt and disappointment. She took her slender volume and went to her room, to try to read like everyone else.

We all loved to read Shevi's books. They had such sweet stories, children's stories that warmed the hearts of adults, too. But my heart ached for her. She was born into a family that gobbled up books like breakfast rolls, and that made the gap between us much more noticeable. I knew that her main problem was coming to terms with Moishy, our baby brother. Moishy is five years younger than the twins, but he was always even more of a bookworm than the rest of us. He even read Esther's and my books!

There was twelve-year-old Shevi who couldn't read six-and-a-half-year-old Moishy's books — a girl who just hated to be different.

"Mommy, why is it hard for Shevi to read?" Bashi asked later. "What does her illness have to do with reading?"

Mommy's face seemed to darken. "It's the dialysis. Shevi's kidneys are barely working and she needs the dialysis, but it weakens her terribly. Her weakness lowers her powers of concentration."

"Well, why can't she stop the dialysis, if all it does is weaken her?"

"Without it, Bashi, her condition would get even worse. But we hope that, with Hashem's help, we'll be able to end those treatments."

"When?" demanded Shevi, appearing suddenly in the doorway. "When?"

Mommy busied herself with clearing the table. She thought a moment, then explained softly, "Shevi, the thing that will help you end the dialysis..." she paused to see how Shevi was reacting, "the only thing...is a transplant."

"A transplant?" Bashi looked at Mommy. I was puzzled, too.

Mommy took out a bar of chocolate and divided it between us.

"Oh, boy! Four squares of chocolate!" Moishy said gleefully.

Mommy continued, speaking slowly. "A transplant means to take a kidney from another person and 'plant' it in place of the sick kidney in the sick person's body."

"What?" cried Shevi in a panic. "They'll put another person's kidney inside of me?" She frowned.

"But that would help you," Mommy said. "Transplanting a new kidney will help you become a new person. You'll feel much better."

"Will it help me...to grow taller?" This was a very sensitive point.

"With Hashem's help, let's hope so."

"Okay! So when can I have the transplant?"

That question was to be repeated many, many times. The news that perhaps she would grow taller excited her, breathed new hope into her. Maybe, just maybe she would finally be like everyone else.

Shevi was embarrassed that she had to ask for help. "No problem, Shevi," I told her. "I'll be only too happy to explain the questions to you."

"I'll never know how to do my homework by myself!" Suddenly the pent-up pain burst forth. "I just don't seem to be very bright! All the other girls understand on their own. I'm the only one who always needs help!"

It was early evening. Shevi had just awakened from her nap. She'd been growing weaker from day to day. Each dialysis treatment sapped her strength further. Her skin, always pale, had turned a yellowish-white once again. I tried to calm her.

"Shevi, you'll see. You'll be able to understand the lessons, too. You're smarter than all the girls in your class — you should know that!"

She seemed skeptical.

"Look, Shevi. After I explain the questions, do you understand them?"

"Yes."

"You see? Even the biggest genius couldn't do homework by herself if she were missing from school three days a week or more!"

"But...."

"But nothing!" I insisted. "You were going to say, 'But I was there for this class.' Right?"

"Yes...."

"So how can you understand what's going on in one class when you're absent for every other one? If it were that simple, the other girls wouldn't come to class every day either. Or the teacher could explain the lesson once, at the beginning, and the girls could do the rest at home!" I took a deep breath and looked sadly at Shevi.

"Even when you are in class, you're so weak you can hardly concentrate. It's the dialysis...it weakens you."

"Yehudis," she answered, gazing at me with those gorgeous, green eyes, "you can't imagine how much I want that transplant."

She looked down at her notebook. All she wanted was to be able to do her homework like everyone else. Such a small thing, yet none of us ever thinks about how blessed we are to be able to do it by ourselves.

The days passed and Shevi was still waiting for notification of the availability of a kidney. She was growing thinner and weaker, and her face had lost every vestige of color.

"That doctor is just...just no help at all!" exclaimed Shevi one morning. "I'll bet he's not even thinking of putting me on the waiting list! Every week, he gives us another story." She stamped a tiny foot on the floor. "And I want to go to school! I'm fed up with missing classes all the time. I wish I knew what's going on!"

We were all sitting around the kitchen table eating breakfast. We sat in silence after her outburst, knowing she was right.

The week before the doctor had said she must become a little stronger before she'd be put on the waiting list. Even then, she felt, she'd be the last on the list. Her patience was really exhausted. None of the children on dialysis seemed to get stronger — only weaker.

Abba finally turned to Mommy and said quietly, "Hannah, she's right. I'm also beginning to think they're stalling." He stirred a spoonful of sugar into his cocoa.

"But what can I do?" Mommy asked with pain in her voice.

"Put pressure on the doctor," Abba answered. "Tell him we have no more patience."

Abba sipped his cocoa. Mommy got up to make our sandwiches to take to school. They seemed calm, both of them, but we knew a storm was raging in their hearts.

Shevi's condition was terrifying us all. Sometimes I would wake up at night from a dream that Shevi had had her transplant operation, that she'd grown as tall as the rest of us, that she was walking along with Bashi, her twin, and people were asking, "Which one is which?" and the twins would smile smugly at each other....

Then I'd wake up and look at Shevi's bed. The sight of her thin, tiny body lying under the covers would return me abruptly to reality.

CHAPTER ELEVEN

A STIFF NECK

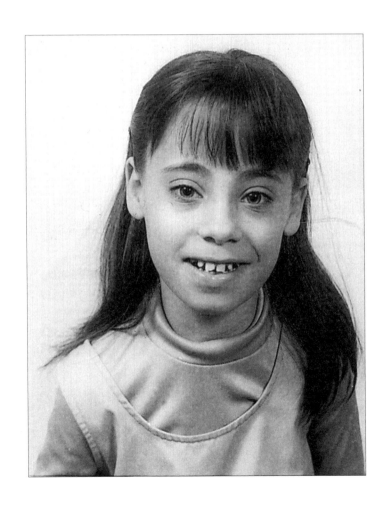

ea ea

"What did you say?" Shevi asked again.
"Nothing. Really, it wasn't anything special," Chaya answered.

Brachi, Chaya, Adina, and Shevi were walking down the street. It was a beautiful, sunny Shabbos afternoon and the girls were on their way to a meeting of the regular Shabbos afternoon groups. The girls met according to classes, each class led by a counselor, an older girl who prepared a program for them to participate in every week.

It bothered Shevi that Chaya would not explain herself or repeat what she had said. Although she walked along beside the others, they towered over her.

"Never mind," Chaya said, looking at the others meaningfully. "You wouldn't understand."

Shevi was really upset now. *Why,* she thought to herself, *do they assume I won't understand? Do they think just because I'm so small my intelligence is undersize? Why won't they understand that I'm just like everyone else inside? I like to know what's going on, I enjoy jokes just like they do, I'm affected by moving stories, too. And I can get angry when someone isn't nice!* As tears gathered in her eyes, she thought to herself it was lucky that her classmates were so absorbed in themselves that they wouldn't notice her discomfort. But Chaya did notice something.

"So, Shevi, what's new with you?"

After being ignored so long, Shevi was surprised by the sudden question and didn't answer.

"Uh-oh! I think she's insulted," Chaya said to her friends, as if Shevi were deaf.

"Have you studied for the Chumash test yet?"

"Is Bashi coming today?"

"How come you left school early yesterday?"

They started to fling questions at her. Shevi carefully answered all their questions, holding back her anger and attempting to keep the annoyance from showing on her face.

Why do they always have to interrogate me? she thought to herself. *Why can't they have normal conversations and talk about the same things they talk about with everyone else?* She felt the tears rising and her throat closing again.

Fortunately they had arrived at the school where the Shabbos programs were held. They met other girls at the door and exchanged greetings, but Shevi barely answered the others and went in with her head held high. *So what if they think I'm stuck-up. Let them for once realize that I'm not a little girl, tagging along with them to their activities.*

Ruchi, the counselor, came in and went right to the center of the crowd. She smiled cheerfully and looked around at the group over Shevi's head, more or less ignoring Shevi. "So what's new?" she asked.

Everyone started to talk at once, telling Ruchi about the latest school project, new babies, family trips. Ruchi listened with interest and commented enthusiastically, not noticing that Shevi stood apart from the others in silence.

"Isn't she the greatest?" Rina whispered to Gila.

"Who's so great?" Shevi boldly asked Rina.

"Why, Ruchi, of course." Rina answered.

Shevi naturally made no comment, but she gazed at the tall, attractive counselor speaking so animatedly to the others and thought to herself, *She doesn't even know I exist. She never looks at me and hardly ever speaks directly to me. I don't think she's so great! Sure, she is charming and attractive and makes a nice impression. But I don't think she's so smart.*

They stood there chattering and gossiping for another ten minutes or so, completely ignoring Shevi, assuming that she had nothing to tell them, not dreaming there was a lot they could learn from her. All they had to do was look down a bit....

To Shevi those ten minutes seemed an eternity. It hurt her to stand so long, and she had a stiff neck from craning up to see and straining to hear what was being said.

"All right, girls, it's getting late. Let's go in and sit down," Ruchi said.

The girls quickly arranged the chairs in a circle and took their seats. Shevi sighed in relief and sat down next to Ruti, whom she hoped would be friendly.

"Who wants to lead us in *minchah*?" Ruchi asked.

Several hands shot up, including Shevi's, but as usual one of the other girls was chosen. Shevi nursed her hurt in silence, wondering why she was never chosen. *Doesn't she know I know the tefillos just like everyone else? Does she think my voice is too weak?* Shevi prayed intently as she always did, sending her prayers upward to the Creator of the universe. In those moments she was the same as everyone else and perhaps better.

The quiz game began. Ruchi had some really interesting questions prepared and the girls vied with each other to be called on, knowing that Ruchi was pleased when they answered correctly. Shevi was invited to answer only once, and it seemed to her as if the counselor couldn't wait for her to finish so she could call on another girl. It seemed to her that Ruchi bestowed a friendly smile upon all except her and hardly ever looked at her. The quiz ended and the girls rushed to the sink outside the classroom to wash their hands for *seudah shelishis*. They told each other contentedly how clever Ruchi was and how much they had enjoyed the quiz.

Shevi followed them, walking slowly and asking herself

why she had come. She was only too aware of girls from other groups eyeing her, pitying her. She even heard their whispered comments. "Look! She's all alone; she has no one to talk to!" A feeling of intense isolation washed over her.

I really should not have come, she told herself. *Every week, it's just the same. I decide I won't come, then Brachi comes to get me with such a nice smile. And while I'm trying to figure out how to refuse, Mommy pushes me to go. Mommy looks so happy that someone has come for me that I just can't argue with her and refuse to go. Then I go down with Brachi, and at first everything is fine with just the two of us walking along and talking as equals, until Adina and Chaya show up! Then they all forget I'm there and I am ignored again. Every week it's the same thing!*

Finally Shevi was allowed near the sink. She was always last because everyone else hurried and pushed and shoved. Didn't it occur to them she was just as hungry as they? When she finally returned to the classroom, everyone was already sitting down and chewing away on slices of bread, some spread with chocolate, some with hummus, some with mayonnaise.

"Oh, Shevi, I'm sorry," said Brachi. "We already said *hamotzi,* and there's no *lechem mishneh* left for you!" There was, in fact, only one slice of bread left on the tray. Brachi apologized, explaining that they hadn't waited for her because one isn't allowed to wait a long time between washing and eating bread. She noticed that all the girls had two or three slices of bread on their napkins while Shevi had only one. "Here, take one of mine," she offered.

"No, thank you. I only need one," said Shevi proudly, although she was really quite hungry. She slowly chewed her slice of bread, just waiting for the program to come to an end so she could go home.

CHAPTER TWELVE

TOWERING SOUL

ॐ ॐ

"Shevi, you have a phone call," Mommy said.

Slowly, Shevi stood up. Her thin legs were aching, but her eyes were glowing. Yes, in this she was like everyone else. She had good friends, caring friends, who phoned her and included her in their lives. I watched as she talked. Her face was animated; the conversation flowed. Shevi took such an interest in everything going on around her. How good it was to see her happy. I fell into a reverie as I sat there, thinking.... What else could we do to make her happy? When would she receive the transplant? Shevi's voice brought me back to the present.

"Yehudis, what are you dreaming about?"

"About...about your transplant," I stammered.

She wrapped her tiny arms around my neck and gave me a hug. "We have to pray hard," she said.

"May the big day be nigh,
when Hashem makes me grow high!"

Shevi had started to make up rhymes, and she loved to compose couplets as she spoke.

"My little poet!" I returned the hug emotionally. "You're so talented!"

She smiled shyly and confessed, "You know, on the telephone, I feel like everyone else. I don't have to stretch my neck and look up high to understand what's happening. And my friends don't have to bend down to see how the 'little one' is getting along!"

"Excuse me," the portly woman asked. "Do you know where the midget who's in sixth grade lives?"

Tovah Leah turned in fury. "Are you talking about my sister?"

Tovah Leah expected the woman to turn red with shame. No such thing! The woman took a white card out of her purse and calmly handed it to Tovah Leah.

"Here's an invitation to my daughter's bas mitzvah party," she said. Noticing Tovah Leah's expression, she added, "They're in the same class."

"My sister's name is Batsheva!" Tovah Leah said with difficulty, a large tear rolling down her cheek. *If only people would stop to think! Why do they call her names? At home we don't even notice that she is so small. If they would only realize what a wonderful person she is, how wise and kind, what a great soul she has.*

"Oh, Lord, let her have her operation, soon," Tovah Leah prayed. "Let us merit seeing her healthy...and tall!"

"Do you need anything else from the store?" Shevi called out.

"Just what's on the list," Mommy answered.

Shevi took the shopping basket and headed for the grocery store nearest the house. As she walked along, she looked over the shopping list. Suddenly she heard a shout:

"Hey!
See the little midget, walking down the street!
She's going shopping, ain't that sweet?"

Shevi stopped short, stunned and shaken. Then she continued on her way.

Walk quickly, but don't run, she told herself. *Don't pay any attention to them, don't cry, keep going.* She held back the tears, raised her head proudly, and kept on walking.

When she reached the grocery store, she hastily piled a few things into the shopping bag, paid the bill, and started for home, walking as quickly as she could.

She heard a different voice shouting at her:

"See the little midget, with the teeny-weeny legs.
She went to the store to buy some eggs!"

This time Shevi didn't pause, even for a second, until she reached home.

I won't tell Mommy, she said to herself. *She'll be so hurt if I tell her. I'll have to be strong and keep it inside.* Shevi knew how hard it would be to try to fool Mommy, for they had an especially close, strong relationship. She usually told Mommy absolutely everything.

"Here are the cookies," Shevi called out as she opened the door.

"Great!" exclaimed Bashi, as everyone came running to the kitchen.

"We were all dying for a treat to go with a good, cold glass of milk," I told Shevi.

With a flourish, Shevi removed the cookies from the basket and set them on the kitchen table.

"Listen to what I say. Bring the milk right away!" Shevi said in rhyme. "Everyone see the treat and please take her seat!"

"Right away, honored poetess! We'll make a bow, and sit down now!"

Shevi was full of fun as always. Her behavior was the same as usual, her jingles adding to the general good humor. We had no idea that anything had happened to her. Until the phone rang....

"Yehudis, Yedida wants to speak to you," Mommy told me.

"Hi, Yedida," I said happily into the phone. "I was going to call you in a little while." I settled down comfortably in the orange chair next to the telephone. Yedida was my best friend and I expected the conversation to be a long one.

"Tell me," she asked abruptly, "was Shevi crying just now?"

I repeated her question in consternation. "Shevi, crying? You don't know Shevi. She never cries, even when she's in pain. She holds out against the most excruciating pain without crying. Why should she be crying now?"

"She wasn't crying?" asked Yedida in astonishment. "Then maybe she was nervous?" the strange interrogation continued.

"Why are you asking all these questions?"

"I was just downstairs on an errand for my mother. Just as I went into the building next store, I heard a little boy's voice calling out, 'See the little midget, with the teeny-weeny legs. She went to the store to buy some eggs!'

"I looked around and saw that the kid shouting at Shevi. I was so upset! I didn't want Shevi to see that I had heard, so I withdrew into the building and peeked out. Shevi just kept on walking, ignoring him, as if nothing had happened. I know she heard him. I felt like going over and slapping him, but I didn't want Shevi to know I'd heard."

"Oh, Yedida! How awful! Until now they called her 'the big baby....'" I choked back my tears. I couldn't say anything else; I was afraid my voice would betray me, and I certainly didn't want the family to hear. Eventually Yedida hung up.

I hurried to the bathroom to wash my face and calm down. When I felt that I could speak again, I called her back.

"What happened?" she asked me.

"You won't believe this, Yedida, but Shevi is acting as if nothing happened. No one could guess she's upset. She must have made up her mind not to say anything about it. It's just like her not to want to cause us aggravation!"

"She is absolutely unbelievable!" Yedida said with admiration.

I blew my nose. "Yes," I said proudly. "That's our Shevi! A towering soul in a tiny body!"

CHAPTER THIRTEEN

LET'S TRY PARIS!

è❧ è❧

*T*hirteen-year-old Shevi was lying in bed in the children's
ward of Shaarei Tzedek hospital — again. The shunt that
had been inserted into her arm to facilitate dialysis was clogged,
and the only way to clear it was with another medical procedure. We were accustomed by now to visiting her in the ward, to
the drab hospital gowns she had to wear, and we even knew
many nurses by name.

The operation was scheduled for the next day and the
twins' good friend Ricki had come to visit, bringing a colorful
package with a yellow paper butterfly pasted on top.

"Thanks, Ricki." Shevi smiled appreciatively and the girls
were soon deep in conversation. They laughed together companionably, much the same as they did at home when they sat
together doing homework on the sofa in our living room. Ricki
was always a loyal and faithful friend. She helped Shevi through
the most difficult times, of which there were many, and was always willing to help Shevi with schoolwork.

Shevi opened the cabinet next to her bed. It was packed
with treats and presents. "Sometimes this whole business pays,"
she said with a wink. She had candies and chocolate bars of all
kinds, a musical pencil box, colored markers, pens that wrote in
irridescent ink, and more. Yet I knew she would have given it all
up to be tall like her friends. Not very tall; just a normal height,
even a bit on the short side, would have sufficed.

The hospital guard walked over to the bed and announced,

"Visiting hours are over. You'll have to leave."

"Good luck!" Ricki said.

"Good luck to you too, on the test!" Shevi said, not forgetting the test she would miss in school the next day. "And...thanks again!"

We had set the alarm to ring earlier than usual the next morning. By 5:00 A.M. we were dressed, Mommy had left for the hospital, and Abba was in shul at the early minyan. We needed the extra time to recite *Tehillim* and pray for the success of Shevi's latest operation. We also prayed that she have the transplant she'd been waiting so long for, soon, and that she be healthy, healthy, healthy!

"Yehudis, please go this afternoon and relieve Mommy at the hospital," Esther told me. "I can't because I'm going to a party tonight."

I didn't ask her why she was going to a party. In our family, we did not change our life around because of an operation. Abba and Mommy insisted that we go to every party or program or happy event together with the girls in our class.

"We'll manage," Abba would tell us, and anyone else who voiced astonishment that we'd go to a party while Shevi was in the hospital.

"Yehudis will be there tonight and Esther will take over tomorrow," he said.

Our parents saw to it that we never felt left out of things because we had an invalid sister. Things were always lively in our home; friends came to visit and we were constantly coming and going. We never felt we were bearing a burden too heavy for us, or that Mommy and Abba were overworked. We loved Shevi with all our hearts, and prayed with her that she would one day be like everyone else.

I reached the hospital at four o'clock in the afternoon. Mommy looked exhausted and I begged her to go home and get some sleep. She straightened Shevi's sheets, covered her with a blanket, and kissed her fondly. "Bye, sweetheart," she said tiredly, and left.

Shevi lay there with one arm securely bandaged, resting on the bed; the other arm was attached to an intravenous tube nearby.

"How are you?" I asked tenderly.

"*Baruch Hashem*...all right," she answered weakly, trying to smile at me. I saw that she was in great pain, but of course she would not complain. As usual, she showed her concern for us. "How are you...managing at home...without Mommy all day? And how is...school?"

I sat by the side of the bed and told her about everyone, all the while watching her bite her lips in pain.

Her doctor entered the room, together with a nurse, and approached the bed. He nodded his head at me and smiled down at Shevi, removing his glasses. "Hello, Shevi."

Shevi stopped biting her lips. She lay there and looked up peacefully at the doctor as though she were just lounging about in bed for no good reason.

"Look at that!" the doctor said to the nurse. "She's got to be in pain, but she acts as if nothing is bothering her."

"Is anything hurting you?" asked the nurse.

"Everything is just fine," Shevi answered.

"I don't understand," the doctor said. "It must hurt...unless you didn't have the operation yet! In that case, we'll take you back to the operating room, all right?" He watched Shevi and waited for her to react, but she fastened her enormous green eyes on him and said nothing.

Shevi did not like to talk to doctors. She seemed to feel it was enough she had to listen to them! She apparently harbored a deep anger toward them and would not speak, would not open up to them, would not complain, no matter how much she suffered.

A week or so later, Shevi had returned to her usual routine.

When she returned from school each day, though, she was exhausted and went straight to bed.

"There's a party tonight," Shevi told Mommy one afternoon.

"Rest up a little," Mommy advised, "and then go."

"What...about my homework?" It was her constant concern. "When will I be able to make up what I've missed?"

"Tonight," I interjected. "I'll help you when you get back from the party."

She went in to rest. She was debilitated because the dialysis was sapping her remaining strength.

Later, Mommy tried to wake her, but Shevi refused to get up. "Mommy, I can't."

"Shevi, try!"

"Mommy, I can't even sit up," she said with her eyes closed.

Mommy was disappointed. She had wanted Shevi to go out and enjoy herself, to be happy, to get out of the house. We all tried to encourage her to get up, but nothing could tempt her — she simply could not get up.

When Shevi said she had no strength, we knew it must be true, as she never used her weakness as an excuse. We had to let her rest.

Abba was highly concerned. "Maybe we should fly to France," he suggested.

"I can't stand seeing her like this!" Mommy agreed. "I feel so helpless. Her condition just keeps getting worse! You're right — I think we have to do something right away!"

"I think we should fly to France and sign up for a transplant there," Abba said firmly. They were both conversant with most of the medical ramifications of Shevi's illness by now.

"I think so, too," Mommy answered. "It will have to be soon, though, or she might not be strong enough to undergo an operation."

Abba went directly to the telephone on his desk in the kitchen and placed several phone calls. For the next two weeks, it seemed he was constantly talking on the phone. Finally he came home one evening and asked Shevi, "What do you say about flying to France the day after tomorrow?"

We immediately became excited, except for Shevi who, in her practical way, wanted first to know why.

"The chances are better in France for a kidney match, since their transplant institute is more advanced," Abba explained.

Mommy's first cousin was the renowned tzaddik, the Pshevorsker Rebbe, Reb Yaakov Leizer, widely and fondly known as Reb Yankele of Antwerp. Abba made arrangements for them to fly to Belgium and spend Shabbos in Antwerp with the Rebbe Reb Yankele and the Rebbetzin in order to arrive at the hospital in Paris early in the morning on Sunday.

One of Reb Yankele's sons-in-law promised to contact the hospital directly and arrange for an interpreter to receive them when they arrived.

Shevi would be examined and tested as an outpatient and, if all went well, she would be put on the institute's waiting list to receive a kidney transplant as soon as possible.

"Have a good flight! May everything go well!"

We hugged and kissed Shevi at the airport. She and Abba would take off in another hour. Shevi was dressed in a smart, olive-green suit, with a matching handbag and olive-green barrettes in her wispy hair. She seemed content. She waved her tiny hand and started to walk toward the escalator — a small, thin figure, with one all-embracing desire: to be healthy and of normal size like everyone else.

Shevi and Abba entered the hospital in Paris early Sunday morning. Everyone around them was chattering away in French. Though Abba's French was not quite up to it, he tried to explain things to the receptionist. She was expecting them, however, and said that the interpreter would soon be along to help them.

It was an uncomfortable fifteen-minute wait, nevertheless,

until a tall young man in a navy suit, accompanied by a short, older, but amiable-looking man in a white coat, approached them. The young man introduced himself and the older man and proceeded to interpret for them. The older man was the head of the transplant institute. He told them that all was " admirably arranged" and that Shevi would be admitted and begin her tests immediately.

"Thank you," said Abba. "And what about the dialysis she needs in the meantime?"

"Oh, yes," the doctor said. "We'll be connecting her to a machine in about thirty minutes."

In Paris, dialysis is done in bed, not in a reclining chair. So Shevi was back in a hospital bed — this time in France, with Abba sitting nearby. A smiling nurse came to take a blood sample and spoke to Shevi in French. Shevi gave her a puzzled look and answered in English. That ended the conversation!

Meanwhile another nurse came in and started up the dialysis machine and a third nurse connected the tube to the shunt in Shevy's arm. Still another nurse presented herself and inquired if they might not like to have lunch at her home after the tests. Although she was Jewish and her invitation was warm and sincere, they could not accept it because they did not know her religious standards. Abba expressed his appreciation.

"Abba, would you give me a pen, please?" Shevi reached for her handbag with her free hand and removed the postcard she had been given on the plane: a picture of an airplane with the name of the airline printed across the top in gold. She took the four-color pen Abba gave her, set it to write in black ink, and filled in the postcard slowly, somewhat hampered by being able to use only one hand.

Dear Bashi,

Shalom! I am writing to you first. Why? I don't know why. I'm in the hospital in Paris, attached to a dialysis machine. The machine here is much bigger, and it looks different. Abba is sitting beside me. He looks tired. I don't want him to know it, but the treatment here hurts me very, very much. It hurts much more than in Eretz Yisroel. But you know me; instead of moaning and grumbling, I decided to write to you. It really, really hurts.

Love,
Your twin sister Shevi

That evening, Abba brought Shevi back to Antwerp to rest up a bit. She was warmly welcomed and cosseted by the Rebbetzin, that wonderful, warm-hearted woman of *chesed* who only regretted that she couldn't communicate with Shevi directly — she spoke neither Hebrew nor English!

In the meantime, Abba got around to confirming their return flight, only to learn that their reservations were no longer available. But Shevi had to be in Israel the next day to continue her dialysis. What should they do?

Fortunately, Abba was acquainted with the manager of Sabena Airlines who, *baruch Hashem*, was able to get them on another flight. "Man plans, but only Hashem decides!"

The next day, Shevi returned home loaded with gifts she had bought in the Brussels air terminal. For Esther and me she had a set of writing supplies — stickers, a stapler, paper clips, and pens, all packed together in a cute, compact little box; for Bashi, a gold-painted necklace pen; for Moishy a gold metallic pen; for Mommy, a watch with a silver-plated watchband. She had also bought a pretty pen for Tovah Leah and other nice gifts for her best friends.

Shevi's green handbag was crammed with snacks and packets of yellow cheese they had bought in Belgium. (Abba told us that Shevi had hardly eaten a thing during the whole trip, and he had been so worried that he tried to tempt her with snacks.)

"Well, you know the dialysis ruins her appetite," Mommy commented sadly.

While Shevi waited to hear from Paris about a transplant, she had to continue her dialysis treatments three times a week, as before. Mommy took her in a taxi because she was simply too weak to travel by bus. "It costs fifteen shekels a day," she explained to Abba.

Abba sighed, but said nothing. He made himself a cup of coffee, took it into his study, and sat down to learn Torah. What was there to say?

CHAPTER FOURTEEN

COUNT YOUR BLESSINGS

❧ ❧

"**H**ow are you feeling, Gila?" Shevi asked a little girl of about eight who was sitting in a wheelchair.

Gila raised very dark, long-lashed eyes and looked at Shevi. "Are you really interested?" she asked bitterly.

"Of course I am! What's bothering you?" Shevi drew nearer to Gila, dragging along her intravenous stand. "Come on, dear, let's go for a little walk."

"I can't...I don't have any strength," Gila answered despairingly.

"Oh, please! Do me a favor. I don't have anyone to walk with me!"

"Do you mean it? I'll be doing you a favor?" Gila perked up and smiled shyly. "I was afraid you were just feeling sorry for me, and that's why you wanted me to go for a walk with you."

"Come on! I don't see what there is to be glum about. All of us here are people 'to be sorry for' — each of us has a different problem." Shevi fixed her green, long-suffering eyes on Gila. Shevi had been hospitalized once again to have the shunt in her arm cleaned out.

The two girls went for a "walk" down the corridors of the children's ward — Gila expertly operating her wheelchair and Shevi dragging along her squeaking intravenous stand.

They studied the paintings on the walls. Shevi stopped in front of one depicting blue skies, sun, trees, green grass, and a house. "Isn't it a lovely picture? Devora painted it," she told

Gila. "May her memory be for a blessing."

"What...happened?" Gila asked.

"Devora had a kidney problem. Like me. She was dependent on dialysis, too. She wasn't allowed to drink water. She wasn't allowed to do a lot of things that I am allowed to do." A tear fell from Shevi's eye.

"One morning, Devora decided she just had to have a cup of hot cocoa. She had a wonderful time making the cocoa. She took a teaspoon, filled it with fresh cocoa powder, and added it to the glass of hot water. She stirred it slowly, lovingly, and added a teaspoon of sugar...." Shevi stopped.

She was remembering a little girl with light brown hair and blue eyes. The image of Devora, of blessed memory, appeared before her. Shevi sighed softly, "Dear Devora!"

"Well?" Gila spoke softly, too. "Go on."

"Yes. Devora stirred the cocoa and sugar into the hot water. She looked so happy. Then she added some milk." Shevi took a deep breath. "Then she drank it.

"Suddenly she put her hand to her head and said the room was spinning around. She fainted; her family called an ambulance as fast as they could. The whole thing was over in a minute. She...died."

Shevi could not hold back her tears. She studied the blue sky in the picture eight-year-old Devora had painted, a sky that matched Devora's blue, blue eyes.

Gila burst into tears. "How awful!"

After a pause, she said thoughtfully, "You know, I always think I'm the most unfortunate person in the world." She studied the small cloud in the painting. "Clouds always seem large to me, but I guess I shouldn't complain. It's just that...it always seems to me that people think that just because I have no legs, I don't have any brains either!"

Shevi smiled at her. "You're certainly not the most unfortunate person in the world, Gila. If you look around you, you'll always find someone with a bigger problem than yours." Shevi paused. "Are you allowed to eat and drink everything?"

Gila nodded her head.

"Always remember those children who would love to enjoy some food or drink like you do. Believe me, there were times when I also felt as if I didn't have enough strength to go on. So I decided to look around me. I discovered that I have a good life! I can drink almost anything I want to, and I have a wonderful family!"

Although tiny in stature and young in years, Shevi spoke like a mature person.

"You're right!" Gila said. "I'll never forget what you told me. I'll try to think of it all the time."

"More than that," Shevi told her with a pat on the back. "You're a smart girl, Gila. It's up to you to teach others that, even if a person is forced to be dependent upon a wheelchair, that person has a healthy, intelligent brain!" Shevi flushed slightly but continued enthusiastically, "You see, those of us who are ill really have two burdens; we have our illness and we have a responsibility to show people that we have brains, that we understand things. It's true it's hard, but it is possible, if we don't give up. Yes, we must not give up!"

Gila regarded Shevi with awe. "Do you know, you sound like a grown-up woman, not a young girl?"

Shevi smiled; Gila's warm words renewed her own courage. If she had succeeded in explaining to this afflicted little girl some of her own feelings, if she had managed to infuse her with some of her own spiritual stamina, she was content. Gila, whose very name embodied the quality she so sadly lacked, joy.

"Always remember, Gila, be full of happiness and joy," Shevi added.

Gila nodded and a huge smile lit her face, a smile of gratitude to the tiny patient from the dialysis ward.

CHAPTER FIFTEEN

BURNING THE MIDNIGHT OIL

S hevi was really distraught. She was in seventh grade and it was examination time. A big test was scheduled in two more days covering all the material they had studied and she had no idea how she was going to catch up on all the work she'd missed. Where should she start? How could she possibly study for the Chumash exam when she didn't understand the Rashi commentary?

"I know it's hard, but you have the brains. If you study, then you'll know." I tried to calm her fears.

"But I can hardly understand the plain meaning, much less the commentary," Shevi answered bitterly. "I'm so stupid!"

"You know that's not true!" I said. "How could you possibly understand everything when you are absent three times a week? Let me ask you something. Do you know what a new baby's name is?"

"What are you talking about?"

"What's my friend Leah's new baby sister's name?"

"How should I know?"

"You must have a low IQ if you don't know," I taunted her.

"Now, wait a minute! How am I supposed to know her name if you didn't tell me?" Shevi asked, surprised into self-defense. "I don't even know Leah!"

"Aha!" I said triumphantly. "That's just what I've been trying to tell you. You don't know Leah, so you don't know her sister's name. If that's clear to you, why isn't it clear that if you weren't in school when a subject was taught, you won't under-stand that subject?"

"Well...maybe." Of course Shevi understood what I was try-ing to tell her. "But do you think it will be enough for me to study it all at home?" She wanted so much to do well at school. Her failure to understand the material distressed her greatly, and it was all reflected in those wise, sad eyes.

"Shevi," I said decisively, "we have two days to study for the Chumash test. I'll help you, and if you study hard, I'm sure you'll succeed."

Shevy was ashamed of her outburst. She dried her eyes and, smiling bravely, hurried to get her Chumash. "I don't have a notebook from class," she explained. Having been absent so much, she hadn't been able to keep her notebook up to date.

"Never mind!" I said confidently. I have no idea where my confidence came from, for she had about two months of mate-rial to absorb in two days. She had to learn basic concepts that ordinarily take years of study. Yet I had faith that she'd succeed. Her wise, intelligent eyes spoke for her. I felt that, with Hashem's help, she would succeed.

We set to work immediately. I made coffee and we sat down at the kitchen table with our rose-colored coffee cups and our books.

"You picked the right color cups for us!" Shevi commented.

I began to explain a Torah principle to her: "An item that is included in a general category, and then mentioned separately in order to teach something, was not singled out to teach only about itself, but to apply its teaching to the entire category...."

The time flew by. Four hours passed and we had only scratched the surface of all the material there was to cover. Shevi again voiced her doubts. I told her she could, and would, do it; it only required willpower.

"Willpower? I have plenty of that. I'm ready to sit here all night if I have to!" Shevi said.

We applied ourselves for another two hours. I explained to her what causes items to become *chametzdik*...and on, and on. At 11:00 P.M. I decided we had studied enough. She needed a chance to absorb what we had gone over before attempting to learn any more.

"You go to sleep," Shevi ordered.

"What about you?" I asked.

"I have to stay here and review all this," she said with determination.

"Maybe you could get up early and go over it in the morning," I suggested.

"All right," she said, after weighing my advice for a few moments. "That makes sense." She hurried to her room, anxious not to waste a minute.

I went to bed exhausted that night. I wasn't used to sitting for so many hours at the books. But Shevi's indomitable will and her iron determination to succeed had spurred me on. As soon as my head touched the pillow, I sank into a deep slumber.

Sometime during the night, I heard a strange noise. I was petrified, thinking someone was trying to break in. I heard another noise and looked at the luminous dial of my clock. It was 4:00 A.M.

"Tovah Leah! Wake up," I whispered, tugging at my sister's arm.

"Wha...what's the matter? What's that noise?" She heard it, too.

"What should we do?" I whispered. We heard papers rustling and a drawer opening and closing. We were both standing up now, shivering and clutching each other in fear. We were sure someone had broken in and was searching Abba's desk.

I wanted to take a peek through the door, to be able to identify "them," but Tovah Leah wouldn't let go of me. She was terrified of burglars.

"Don't you dare go in there," she ordered. Just then we

heard footsteps, clearly. We heard a drawer opening again. Then...silence!

We stood there for at least five minutes, trembling, but heard no further sounds. I tiptoed to the door of our room, but it had opaque glass panels and I couldn't see a thing. Suddenly, I grabbed at Tovah Leah.

"*Imaleh*!" Tovah Leah smothered a scream.

"I just saw a shadow pass the door," I whispered to her. "Let's throw something and make a noise!"

"No! No!" Tovah Leah clung to me.

I banged on the door loudly.

"Oh, no!" Tovah Leah cried. "He...he's coming toward us!"

A voice rang out, "Yehudis? Tovah Leah? What on earth are you doing?" The bedroom door opened.

"Shevi!" We sank down on the floor in relief. "We heard someone wandering around the house and we thought it was a burglar!"

"Just a second," Tovah Leah said. "What on earth are you doing wandering around the house at this hour?" We spoke in whispers; everyone else had so far slept through it all.

"Oh, I'm studying," she answered. "I want to get a good mark in my test. I've been up for an hour and a half." She fastened her huge, green eyes on us.

"And do you understand everything now?" I asked.

"Yes, I do. I've gone over everything you explained to me — you explain things so clearly, Yehudis, and now I understand."

That is how Shevi got through those exams. She would not permit her illness to conquer her; she did not want any allowances made for her. She was determined to succeed on her own, and she invested hours in reviewing the material. We grew accustomed to hearing noises in the night. She knew quite well that others took the exam period in stride with only a bit of extra effort, whereas for her, passing every small quiz was a major undertaking. All our assurances that she was justified in not knowing the material well because she had missed so many classes were in vain. Shevi was not happy with herself unless she could do whatever her contemporaries did. At times her spirits flagged, but she would not let herself weaken, and she drew upon unknown depths of spiritual vigor to revive her determination.

"What mark did you receive on the Chumash exam?" I asked Shevi when she returned from school four days after our marathon study session.

"How did you know it was returned today?"

"I heard your friends talking about it."

"I'd rather not say," she said unhappily.

I stood there for a moment at a loss. Had she failed — after so many hours of study?

"I told you I'm stupid," she said.

"That's not true! I won't let you, or anybody else, say such a thing."

Shevi looked at me sadly. I immediately realized I had not given her a good answer.

"One second...what mark did you get?"

"Well, all right. I'll show you." She opened her schoolbag and I saw that it was wondrously organized: Her books were in neat rows and all the loose papers were in a special section. She withdrew some folded pages and held them out to me.

I took the pages from her and looked them over carefully, praying that I would know the right thing to say. Her name was neatly printed at the top in small letters. The pages were covered with writing, but here and there I saw a blank where an answer was missing. An occasional comment from the teacher was penned in: "Nice answer." "Very good." "Excellent answer."

I hugged Shevi and pointed to these comments.

"Those were easy questions," she said, dismissing my enthusiasm.

I looked through the rest of the exam, seeking the right thing to say to her. At the end I discovered the mark: seventy-eight. "That's wonderful!" I exclaimed.

"What's so wonderful about it? Are you telling me seventy-eight is a better mark than a hundred?" she asked me sarcastically.

It was impossible to fool her. Nevertheless I really meant it. "Shevi, seventy-eight is a really good mark, even for an ordinary student. And for you, who weren't there for most of the classes, who are physically so weak, who accomplished this all on your own without the teacher's help, why, it's amazing."

A tiny smile hovered on her lips. She grudgingly admitted that I might be right.

"Well, maybe I was expecting too much. I wanted to get a hundred. I really thought I had such a good command of the material."

"You do. A seventy-eight means you have a very good command of most of the material," I said.

I remember that conversation clearly; it was similar to many others we had through the years. Shevi's expectations were high, her will was strong. However tired or sick she felt, she'd draw on her deep spiritual strength to assist her physically. She'd pull herself out of bed, slowly move toward the desk. Her hands, swollen from needle punctures, would turn pages and pages of information, and her extraordinary willpower would keep her at the desk, studying, studying, until she was satisfied.

CHAPTER SIXTEEN

ANOTHER DISAPPOINTMENT

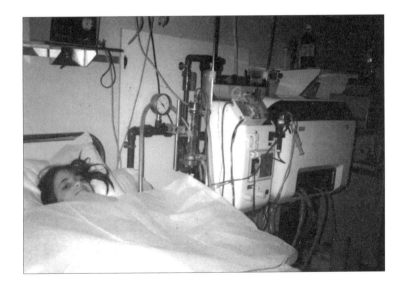

◆ ◆

Whenever the phone rang at an unusual hour, we all listened tensely to the conversation, hoping that finally, finally, it was about a kidney transplant for Shevi. Just before Rosh HaShanah in Shevi's thirteenth year, the ring of the telephone alerted us as we were having lunch together.

"Really?" Mommy said with excitement in her voice. She signaled us to be quiet so she could hear. As she replaced the receiver, her glowing eyes told us the good news.

"There's a kidney available for you, Shevi!" she exclaimed.

We picked little Shevi up and danced around with her in our arms.

"Here's twenty shekels," Mommy said to me. "Go down right now and get us some ice cream cones to celebrate!" I danced more than ran all the way to the grocery store and back.

When we started to unwrap the cones, Mommy suddenly remembered that Shevi had to begin fasting immediately: She wasn't allowed to join in the celebration of her own farewell-to-dialysis party, and perhaps, farewell-to-being-a-small person party, too. As usual, her spirits were high in spite of the prohibition, and she didn't seem to mind watching us enjoying ourselves.

A few hours later, after we had kissed Shevi and wished her good luck, Abba drove her and Mommy to Hadassah Hospital. We all went to the Kosel to pray for her. We were ecstatic in our joy and hope and faith. Soon, soon, we thought, Shevi would be like everyone else; soon she'd be able to eat everything and stop going for four-hour treatments three times a week, and maybe, maybe she'd begin to grow.

When they arrived at the hospital, Shevi was immediately whisked upstairs, dressed in a hospital gown, and connected to a dialysis machine. All the while the nurses were taking blood samples from her. Yes, the kidney was compatible, *baruch Hashem*! "The last treatment," she whispered to herself with deep emotion.

"You'll be taken to the operating room at midnight," the head of transplant surgery told her. Shevi squeezed Mommy's hand, and they both choked back a rush of tears. An end to dialysis! Health and well-being! She'd be a good student just like all her friends! She was about to have the yearned-for operation and receive a new kidney.

Mommy called us early the next morning. She sounded very tired, but she tried to reassure us that everything was probably all right. It was too soon to know anything definite. Nevertheless, we danced and sang and jumped up and down on our beds. Bashi acted out how she and Shevi would be the same height. They would go for a walk and people would not be able to tell them apart. She daydreamed out loud about the tricks they could play on their friends, just like real twins!

"The main thing is that Shevi will be healthy," Tovah Leah reminded us seriously.

Mommy stayed in the hospital all day, phoning us at intervals: when Shevi left the operating room; when Shevi was tucked into her bed in the ward; when Shevi opened her eyes. We rejoiced and anticipated a healthy Shevi's return home. We couldn't wait to watch her eat a banana — a treat which had been forbidden to her for over a year (because of its high potassium content).

Two days passed in high hopes.

On Friday, Abba took us all to the hospital to visit Shevi.

Mommy came with us, as she had left Shevi alone for the first time to come home and organize our meals for Shabbos. In my hand I clutched a bouquet of flowers with a "get well soon" card attached, on which we had signed our names in Day-Glo ink.

We were in such a hurry to see Shevi, and of course to get back home before Shabbos, that we even resented having to wait on line to be checked in by the security guard. Finally we reached her room, but...her bed was empty!

"Where's my daughter?" Mommy cried out in consternation.

The patient in the next bed, also a transplant patient, looked at Mommy enigmatically and said quietly, "They took her for dialysis...."

Mommy rushed out of the room, heading for the dialysis ward. We followed slowly after her and stood outside the dialysis room, hearts pounding in fear. We heard sobbing. It was Shevi, Shevi who never cried in the presence of a doctor, who bit her lips so she would not cry out in pain.

"The transplant didn't take! I still need dialysis!" she wailed. And for once, her crying lasted long into the night.

CHAPTER SEVENTEEN

THE LETTER

&? &?

"No! It's enough! Tomorrow I won't go!" Shevi was exasperated and discouraged with her never-ending dialysis treatments.

"But you must go," Mommy tried to persuade her.

"Why? What will happen if I don't go?" Shevi cried emotionally. "I just get weaker every day anyway! All day long I feel weak and tired. How is it helping me?"

Shevi sat down and continued more quietly, only her eyes broadcasting her pain and unhappiness. "I go to school, I sit in class, and I haven't the strength to pay attention properly." Tears appeared in her eyes. "Can you imagine what it's like to sit through five classes and not be able to concentrate? I feel so weak and exhausted all the time."

She hurried from the room to nurse her unhappiness in private.

The rest of us sat there, not knowing what to say. We were all thinking, *She's right!*

"Mommy!" Shevi suddenly cried, returning to the kitchen. "What about Esther's wedding? I want so much to look nice at Esther's wedding and be happy at her *simchah*. Let me start treatment after the wedding, please!"

"I know what we'll do," Mommy said and put a reassuring smile on her face, one of those smiles that always renewed Shevi's courage. "Let's ask Rav Scheinberg for a blessing!"

The next day at two o'clock, Abba, Mommy, and Shevi entered the elevator of our building and rode up to the top floor, to Rav Scheinberg's apartment. We were fortunate to live in the same building as this great *rav*.

An aura of holiness permeated Rav Scheinberg's study. He listened carefully to their request and, smiling sweetly at Shevi, gave her a blessing that she should look wonderful at her sister's wedding.

His blessing was fulfilled; Shevi was able to attend Esther's wedding and she did look beautiful!

On Sundays, Tuesdays, and Thursdays, Shevi went to Shaarei Tzedek Hospital for dialysis. She returned looking pale and weak and Mommy would tell her to go right to bed. Without arguing, Shevi would do just that, and then sleep for hours on end.

Energetic, enthusiastic Shevi, who, in spite of her illness, had never rested for a minute, had been constantly on the go, was now a weak and sickly girl and needed lots of sleep.

"She's not the same Shevi," Mommy said sadly.

"How much longer can it go on like this?" asked Bashi quietly. "It's terrible to see her sleeping so much. I don't recognize my twin! She gets home from school with barely enough strength to drink a glass of water, and goes straight to bed. She sleeps and sleeps, then tries to do her homework when she wakes up, but even then she is tired and weak."

Bashi paused and looked at us. "I can't believe this is Shevi! She used to be so mischievous; we used to play pranks all the time. Now, when I ask her to go babysitting with me, she just looks at me with mournful eyes and says she's too weak — and I know it's true. She's just getting weaker and weaker...." Bashi burst into tears and hurried from the room.

In the heavy silence that followed Bashi's outburst, we heard someone knocking at the door. Tovah Leah went to answer it and we heard her chatting with someone.

"Call Shevi," she shouted. "It's her friend Michal."

I went in to tell Shevi. She smiled and said it was so nice that Michal had come by, but she really, really could not get up. I urged her to try and held out my hand to help her. Mommy joined us.

"No, I can't. Tell her I'm sleeping," she begged.

"No, Shevi, we can't tell her you're sleeping," Mommy said. "Afterward you'll regret sending your friend away. We can't always say you're sleeping. Try to be strong."

She sat up with our help, stifling a groan. Soon she was standing, leaning against the bed. She called out, "Michal, I'll be right there!" Slowly, she made her way to the living room, her steps growing steadier as she went, and grinned at Michal with satisfaction.

Michal was a staunch friend of many years, who had always encouraged Shevi in good times and bad. She dropped by to visit or phoned Shevi regularly. When we'd thank her for being such a good friend, she'd answer modestly, "I just like to be with Shevi. Believe me, I come for myself because I learn a lot from Shevi."

She was right. It was possible to learn a great deal about life from Shevi; we were pleased Michal had discovered this.

Michal and Shevi sat in the living room and talked. "Did we have a lot of homework tonight?" Shevi asked.

"Didn't you know? We went on a field trip today, " Michal told her.

"No, I didn't know," said Shevi sadly. "They always seem to have trips and outings on the days when I go for dialysis. I think they do it on purpose! I think they are afraid to have me come along on their trips," she added with a trace of anger in her voice.

"I can't believe that," Michal said thoughtfully. Could there be some truth to what Shevi was saying?

"It's interesting that they announced the trip two days ago, when I was in dialysis." Shevi said. "Yesterday Mrs. Levine didn't mention anything about a trip, and today, when I wasn't there, you went."

"It is strange," Michal said under her breath, trying to determine if it was true.

"Did she mention anything in class yesterday? No! Because I was there," Shevi exclaimed triumphantly.

"Just a minute," Michal said hesitantly. "I'm sure I heard her say, 'Remember to bring everything you need tomorrow.' "

"When did she say that? I didn't hear anything like that." Michal tried to remember.

"No, it can't be," Shevi insisted. "I may be a weak student, but I'm not deaf!" They both sat there concentrating, trying to remember.

"Just a minute," Shevi said. "I remember now. I left class half an hour early yesterday. I had to go to the doctor to have my blood pressure checked."

"Yes!" Michal confirmed. "That's right. That's when the teacher 'remembered' to remind us what to bring on the outing." They sat there looking at one another without saying another word.

Mommy came in with a tray of lemonade and cookies. "Why are you sitting there looking at each other?" she asked. "Have you had an argument?"

"No, Mommy. I just discovered I was right about something," Shevi said bitterly. "The class went on a field trip today."

"Today? You never said anything about it."

"That's the point," Shevi said. "The day before yesterday, when I was in dialysis, the teacher announced the trip. Yesterday, she never mentioned a word about it until after I left. I had to go to the doctor and left early." She turned to Michal. "It's lucky that I left early, or you might not have been reminded."

Michal laughed, and they went on talking and enjoying each other's company.

Mommy, however, was not amused. She usually tried not to discuss the many difficulties and problems that accompanied Shevi's illness with any of us. But I was in the kitchen when she came in and I could see something was wrong. She told me what Shevi had said and added, "This business with the class trips is complicated. Maybe they could send you along, since you are their Shabbos counselor now."

"I'd be glad to go," I said. "Every teacher can ask a class counselor to accompany her on trips.

"This is the fourth time Shevi has missed out on a field trip this year," I mused. "I know they had one Biblical-places tour, and once they went to a park to play outdoor games, and...I don't understand why the teacher doesn't just call you and ask if Shevi can participate in the class trips. Do you think there is any risk in taking her? In any case, why don't they call and at least ask?"

I soon came to understand that many people prefer to ignore a problem than to bring it out in the open, in the hope that it will just fade away or solve itself. Perhaps people just don't want to get involved in the problems of others, as if they could "catch" the problem like a disease.

The truth was that many of Shevi's teachers in elementary school "papered over" the fact that they had a girl with a serious medical problem in their class, a girl who was trying her best to fit in and be accepted. These teachers were unable to understand that they were in a position of authority and trust and might have contributed a great deal to lighten a young girl's burden. By their example they might have lessened the sadness and alienation she felt and saved her many tears and much aggravation.

Two more weeks passed without Mommy deciding what to do about the field trips. *Maybe it was just a coincidence,* she thought.

The school secretary poked her head into the classroom, interrupting the lesson. She looked around the room with a smile on her face and, after excusing the interruption, made an announcement: there was to be a class trip the next day. They were going to a national park, an area of great natural beauty. There would be walking trails and streams to cross and plenty of room to play and relax. It was to be a Rosh Chodesh excursion instead of the usual Rosh Chodesh party.

The girls applauded and cheered almost before the secretary had finished speaking. There was such a tumult of excitement and noise that they could barely hear her concluding remarks about taking a picnic lunch and returning home in the afternoon.

Oh, dear! Shevi said to herself. *Another outing — just when I can't go. But why do they have to go tomorrow? This month there are two days of Rosh Chodesh; they could have scheduled it for the day after. Why don't they ever give me a chance to participate? I suppose they assume I can't manage it, or the trails are too difficult for me, or...whatever.* She remained frozen in her seat.

Shira, who was sitting at the next desk, turned to Shevi and asked, "Isn't that great? Aren't you glad? Why aren't you smiling?"

"Um...er...well, yes, sure, it's great."

"Come on, tell me. What were you daydreaming about?" Shira persisted.

"Oh, I...er...was just trying to remember if I know that park...."

"Are you coming then?" Shira insisted.

Shevi really wanted to ask her rudely what business it was of hers and to tell her to please stop bothering her with questions. She didn't want to have to explain.

"Well?" Shira prodded.

"What...difference does it make?" Shevi finally answered.

Shira was startled by Shevi's question. She was not used to hearing Shevi speak sharply. She tossed back her mane of dark curls said, "Well, I surely don't care whether you go or not. It will be your loss, not mine!" And she stood up straight and tall and strode away.

Oh, dear, what have I done? Shevi berated herself silently. *Look who I've picked a fight with. Well, so what? What am I afraid of? Maybe now she'll stop being so nosy and asking me so many questions. The truth is I can't stand their curiosity and pity.*

As the hubbub died down a bit, Shevi's good friend Michal suddenly asked, "What day is tomorrow?"

"Tomorrow is Tuesday," Rina answered with a big smile.

Michal glanced across the room at Shevi and asked herself once again, *Was Shevi right? Do they really plan these trips so that Shevi can't join us?* The thought disturbed her greatly.

Shira happened to notice Shoshi's puzzled expression. "Now Michal is daydreaming, too!" she said with a friendly smile.

Everyone loved Michal. She was a lively girl with a pleasant nature, a good student who could be amusing as well, and she always knew how to make others feel good. Though she was popular and had many friends, she never ignored Shevi. "Shevi, shall we meet after school today?" she would always ask. Shevi truly enjoyed their friendship.

When Shevi returned from school that day, Abba immediately commented on her unhappy look. "Let me guess," he joked. "I'll bet there's a class trip tomorrow — just when you have to go for dialysis!" He was trying to play it down in Shevi's eyes.

"You're right," Shevi said, blushing.

Mommy got up and left the room. In her bedroom, she picked up the phone and, with trembling fingers, dialed the number of the school. Busy! She dialed again. Busy! She kept dialing.

At last she heard the voice of the school secretary saying, "Bais Yaakov; good afternoon."

"May I speak to Mrs. Levine?"

"I'm sorry, she isn't here now."

"May I speak to the principal?" Mommy asked, before she lost her nerve.

Before long the principal was on the phone. "Hello?"

"Yes, this is Shevi Wittow's mother. I want to know why we are being treated this way! Why are all the class outings scheduled on the days that Shevi has to go to the hospital for treatment? Are you afraid the girls will have to walk slower? Are you afraid they will have to cut short their trips because of Shevi?" Mommy took a deep breath and kept going.

"I think that a school ought to be able to give a little...to make a few concessions for a little girl who has such a great burden to bear!" Her voice trembled, but she plunged ahead. "A girl who has to undergo such difficult treatments, who suffers so terribly, ought to be able to have at least a little fun...." Mommy broke off. She could not say any more.

The principal was incredulous. What could she say? She was well aware of Shevi's problems and she sympathized with a mother who had good reason to be upset, a mother who had to travel such a hard road together with her daughter. There was a brief silence on the line.

"Listen," Mommy managed to continue, "I apologize for my outburst. It just hurts so much that my daughter isn't given a chance to...enjoy herself a little...to forget her suffering for a while...."

"I'm glad you called me," the principal said quietly. "I will look into this; I'll talk to Shevi's teacher. I must admit this comes as a complete surprise to me." They spoke a bit longer, Mommy answering the principal's questions, and the conversation ended.

Later that evening, when the younger children were already asleep, Tovah Leah and I were doing our homework in the kitchen while Mommy washed the supper dishes. The phone rang, but Tovah Leah and I were reluctant to pick it up. We were somewhat uneasy because Mommy had been very tense the whole evening and we were afraid it might be bad news.

Mommy answered the phone. "Yes...yes...I understand.... Well, yes, I do have some things to say, but now is not the time. Thank you very much for calling," she said formally.

"Who was it, Mommy?" we asked curiously.

Mommy didn't answer.

"Please tell us. We want to know what's wrong."

Mommy gave in. "It was Shevi's teacher." She told us how she had spoken to the principal about the class trips, and evidently the principal asked Shevi's teacher to call her.

"Well, what did she say?"

"She explained why the class trips always take place on the days Shevi isn't there."

"And...why do they?" we asked.

"I just don't have strength to repeat the entire conversation," Mommy sighed. "There's nothing easier than finding excuses, you know."

We didn't press her further. We packed up our books and went into our bedroom.

Mommy told us afterward that she had continued to sit in the kitchen, staring blankly at the wall. After a while her hand, seemingly of its own accord, picked up a ballpoint pen from the desk and reached for a writing pad. This is what she wrote:

Dear Mrs. Levine,

I want to tell you something. I want you to know that among all the dialysis patients in the world, there are relatively few children. Among those children, few are Jewish. Of those Jewish children who are dialysis patients in Jerusalem, there is only one young girl who is a student at a Bais Yaakov school. Do you realize what a *zechus*, a privilege, that is for all of you at that school? To receive into your midst a marvelous little girl, a little girl who stands tall in wisdom and knows so much about life? Isn't it possible to show some consideration for her suffering, for her travail in undergoing difficult treatments three times a week, every week?

I write to you from an overflowing heart. You must know that a sick child is a test for her parents, for her siblings, for her whole family. And she is also a test of the humanity of the school and its teachers. I hope you remember that!

I would like to give you a blessing that this may be your only test as a teacher, and only as a teacher. May you never suffer such a test in a closer relationship. So please make use of this opportunity and appreciate the merit that you have acquired.

Mommy signed her name, folded the letter, and inserted it into an envelope. Two hot tears fell on the envelope — the tears of a mother who knew how to accept with great love the test that was allotted to her.

CHAPTER EIGHTEEN

SHEVI'S SURPRISE

હૈ≥ હૈ≥

We were all excited and happy: Grandma Wittow was coming from Denver, Colorado, to spend Pesach with us.

"I think we should begin to fix up the apartment now, besides cleaning for Pesach," Bashi said. It was true, the apartment could use a bit of freshening up. We didn't want Grandma to think we were in such dire straits that we couldn't have a nice apartment.

"Well, I don't think material things are as important as spiritual things," Tovah Leah said.

"It's very nice to have a pretty, well-kept house," Shevi piped up. "But there are more important things in life. The main thing is happiness...and health!"

Abba and Mommy smiled at Shevi's earnest pronouncement. Young Shevi could indeed differentiate between essentials and nonessentials; she had a fine sense of values.

"Shevi is right," Abba said. "Not everything that glitters brings happiness. Not every sophisticated appliance and clever gadget brings its user joy. Gadgets and modern appliances are great if they make life easier for us, or more interesting, but if you are not content with whatever you have, the fancy trappings are worthless. And, as Shevi says, without good health, all the material wealth in the world is not important.

"However..." Abba took a deep breath and looked around at us and the apartment. "I admit that with a little work, and maybe a small investment, we can improve things around here."

Over the next two weeks, we all worked hard to get the house ready for Pesach. Abba took care of the structural improvements and Mommy appointed cleaning tasks.

Shevi, who had returned from the hospital only a few days earlier, having undergone more difficult and painful tests, was not about to be left out, weak as she was. She insisted on cleaning Grandma's room all by herself. (The twins' bunk bed was moved into our room, and Grandma would have their room to herself.)

Mommy was always concerned that we not overexert ourselves. Since she was in the hospital with Shevi so often, we girls had taken over many household tasks. I am amazed today when I realize how Mommy always managed to keep our home running so smoothly and normally under very great pressure. Abba, on the other hand, always encouraged us to be original, creative, and active, and to undertake all sorts of enterprises. Even if we sometimes failed (which did happen!), he would tell us not to mind because one can always learn from his or her mistakes.

So Shevi was permitted to clean Grandma Wittow's room by herself...and a wonderful job she did! We were astonished at what she was able to achieve, suffering the discomforts she did. Grandma's room was sparkling, shining, absolutely fit for a queen!

But Shevi had another surprise to spring, of which none of us had the slightest suspicion except her twin Bashi.

Grandma arrived and duly voiced her approval of the newly painted, clean, and shining apartment. After she had moved into her spotless, well-ordered room, and put her things away in the wall closet, Shevi presented her with a shoebox-size package, wrapped in gift paper.

We crowded around, bursting with curiosity. When had Shevi had time to prepare a gift for Grandma? With all the time spent in the hospital, with all the effort she had put into cleaning the room, when on earth had she worked on it? And what could little, weak, sick Shevi possibly have made?

"Don't make such a fuss," Shevi begged us. "It's really not so great." She always modestly tried to disclaim credit; she considered herself and her ideas unimportant.

Grandma unwrapped the gift and opened the box in great suspense. She lifted out a set of white table napkins, delicately embroidered with tiny flowers in beautiful pastel hues. Amid the flowers peeped Grandma's initials in tiny, graceful letters.

"Shevi! These are exquisite!" Grandma said. "However did you find time to do this? What a wonderful present!" She was moved to tears, and took Shevi in her arms to hug and kiss her.

"I just wanted to do something nice for you. You're always sending us nice presents and doing things for us."

Though we had always known how capable Shevi really was, we were nevertheless astonished at her talent and moved by her sensitivity. Her words hung in the air as a lesson for all of us in expressing gratitude.

CHAPTER NINETEEN

WHY THIS PESACH WAS
DIFFERENT

₰ ₰

*T*he house was free of *chametz*, our guest had arrived, the
Pesach dishes were on the shelves in the kitchen, and the
shelves held matzah, potato starch, and other Pesach foods.
That evening Abba would search the house for any crumbs we
might have overlooked, and the evening after we would sit
down to enjoy our Pesach seder.

Shevi and Mommy, however, were in the hospital for a regular dialysis session. A nurse had just taken the usual prelimi-
nary blood sample and was preparing to give Shevi an injection.
The needle was already in Shevi's arm; the nurse had only to at-
tach the ampoule with the medication when the telephone at
the nurses' station across the corridor began to ring. It seemed
no one was there to answer it.

"Don't move, now," the nurse cautioned Shevi. "I'd better
answer the telephone."

Shevi remained motionless, gazing at some point off in the
distance. She seemed indifferent to the needle in her arm, to the
large machine standing next to her chair, to everything going
on around her.

"Really?" they heard the nurse ask, apparently excited.

Shevi turned her head. What could be so exciting in the dialysis ward? Maybe one of the children had suffered a burst
vein; that was not so unusual here. Maybe someone's needle
had shifted and begun to hurt? Maybe someone had gotten
dizzy in the middle of a treatment? Nothing unusual about any

of these things in the dialysis ward. Pain, blood, dizziness, weakness — routine!

The nurse hurried back into the room. "Shevi! Shevi! Mrs. Wittow!" she cried. "I can't believe it! It's a miracle, a miracle for sure, that I didn't give you that injection. And the hypodermic was already in my hand! I was about to connect it to the needle — why, another second, and you would have missed out!"

"Missed out on what?" Mommy asked.

"A transplant!" the nurse cried.

The nurse was gratified to see a small smile appear on Shevi's wan face.

"Of course, it has to be tested to see if it is compatible for you. We'll have to do more blood tests. But if it is compatible and if I had given you the injection, we wouldn't be able to get an accurate reading of your blood test for hours." She looked gravely at the fragile figure with the needle stuck in her arm. "And if we had had to wait for several hours for the results of the blood test," she continued as she removed the needle from Shevi's arm, "it might have been too late to receive the transplant! Well, we'll know in an hour." She shook her head in wonder.

Mommy rose from her chair and went to telephone Abba at home. As she dialed, she noticed the light of a small lamp glowing in the gloom of the nurses' station in the shadowed corridor. She smiled to herself and thought, *A light in the darkness. With Hashem's help....*

Abba turned from the telephone and announced to the room at large, "When I'm searching for *chametz* tonight, guess where Mommy will be?"

We all made wild guesses except for Bashi, who with a twin's intuition said with certainty: "I know! A transplant — Shevi's going to have a transplant!"

"How did you know, Bashi?" Abba asked her.

"I just saw how happy you were, Abba, and I knew. What else could make you so happy except a transplant for Shevi?"

I hugged Bashi and kissed her, but none of us jumped for joy this time. No one ran to the store to buy ice cream and no one danced around the room. We knew too well all that was involved. We were filled with suspense and trepidation.

"How about a cup of coffee for everyone?" Esther asked, knowing as usual what to do at a difficult time. Esther had been married shortly before Pesach that year, and she had come to help us with the cooking. Mommy had only prepared the gefilte fish, and nothing else was ready.

Esther proceeded to make a pot of coffee in the *Pesachdik* coffeemaker and poured us each a cupful to drink.

"Is there a match?" Grandma asked, taking a sip.

"They are doing the final tests right now," Abba answered, inhaling and exhaling deeply. "If all goes well, the operation will be tonight!"

"But tonight is *bedikas chametz*," I reminded everyone. "What should we do?"

"Do?" asked Abba. "Why, we'll do just what the halachah tells us to do. We'll search for *chametz.*

"And just think how carefully Shevi is going to be observing the laws of Pesach!" he continued with unquenchable optimism. "Most people just buy new dishes and pots for Pesach. Shevi is going to get a whole new kidney! A kidney that will take all the impurities out of her body and clean her blood before Pesach!"

Shevi had indeed always been particular about Pesach cleaning. The room she shared with Bashi always shone with a special radiance and cleanliness. How she had cleaned it for Grandma this year, despite her weakness. Every inch of the room was polished and shining; whatever could be laundered was freshly washed and ironed; the pictures sparkled in their frames; there wasn't a particle of dust or dirt to be seen. Of course, it had taken her many hours and days to do it, but she had done it. We admired her so!

And perhaps that devotion to halachah would stand in her merit, perhaps this time the operation would be a complete success. Maybe her extraordinary care in removing *chametz* from her presence would ensure that she would not have any *chametz* within her either, and her new kidney would filter out all the impurities that had made her so sick.

We went to the Kosel that evening to pray for Shevi. We sent aloft our most heartfelt prayers to the Creator of the world. With the tears flowing unchecked down our cheeks, we beseeched Hashem to make the operation a success.

Bashi added her own prayer, "May Shevi now be like everyone else."

Tovah Leah prayed, "May she grow quickly."

We shivered in the wind, whether from cold or from emotion, I don't know. We murmured our prayers over and over again.

We returned home close to midnight and awaited the telephone call from Mommy. Shortly after we arrived, she called to say Shevi still hadn't been taken to the operating room.

Esther had joined us at the Kosel with her husband and returned home with us. We discussed what we should do: there was still lots of cooking and baking to be done, and we knew Mommy must be doubly worried.

"Esther will help us," I said confidently. She was a bundle of energy and we knew we could count on her. How many times had she surprised us with a cake she had baked or something special she had cooked, just when we needed it. Shevi had even made up a rhyme about her: "When Esther's here, have no fear; worry and tension disappear!"

"Yes, of course I'll help," Esther said, smiling in agreement. "But even though we'll all pitch in, the main burden is Mommy's."

The phone interrupted our discussion and I picked it up. "Hello, Mommy, what's going on?"

"They hope to take her down to the operating room in half an hour. She's already connected to an intravenous setup and is all ready."

"I'll tell everyone."

"Pray!" Mommy begged me. "Everyone pray!" She broke off.

Twenty-five minutes later, she called again. "They wheeled her into the operating room seven minutes ago. Pray!"

"We are praying!"

Abba returned from the hospital at two o'clock in the morning. "You must all go to sleep," he said when he saw us. "Tomorrow night will be seder night, and we all have a lot to do tomorrow."

Reluctantly, we stood up, one by one, and slowly went off to our beds, but I don't think any of us expected to sleep much. All our thoughts and prayers were with Shevi.

CHAPTER TWENTY

SEDER NIGHT

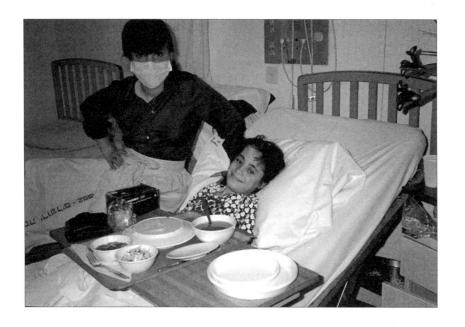

૨૭ ૨૭

I opened one eye and realized the sun was flooding the room with daylight. It was already morning!

My thoughts immediately turned to Shevi. Quickly I opened both eyes, sat up, and looked around at my sisters, slumbering peacefully in their beds.

"Girls! Get up! We have to get ourselves organized. It's *erev Pesach* today." Not a rustle. "Let's go find out how Shevi is," I said, trying a different tack. That did it. Bashi and Tovah Leah sat up immediately.

"We've been lying here asleep, while Mommy's been sitting up all night outside the operating room!" said kindhearted Bashi.

We could all picture it, Mommy sitting on an uncomfortable chair all night long saying *Tehillim*, praying for Shevi to recover from the operation, for the transplant to "take," and for Hashem to help her little girl. We could only hope and pray that her prayers would be answered.

"Come on," I said, "let's get moving. We have so much to do today."

And we did it. We divided up the work; no one argued, no one objected to doing anything she was asked to, and our fingers flew from task to task. We made *charoses*, we roasted chickens, we ground nuts, we peeled potatoes and carrots, Grandma baked Pesach cakes. Yet all the while we were expecting the telephone to ring with news of Shevi.

The front door opened; Mommy was back! Grandma hurried in from the dining room, where she had been setting the table for the seder. Esther's husband came in from the balcony, where he had been kashering some glassware. We plied Mommy with questions, all with the same intent: How was Shevi?

Eight-year-old Moishy had more sense than all of us put together. "Let Mommy sit down," the clever child said. "Give her a cup of coffee, Esther."

Mommy drew Moishy toward her and hugged him. "Thank you, Moishy dear...thank you for worrying about me."

Mommy had huge black shadows under her eyes; she was pale and exhausted. It was apparent that she hadn't slept all night. We quieted down and waited for her to drink her coffee and collect herself.

Bashi couldn't hold back the question we were all longing to ask: "Tell us just one thing, please, Mommy. Tell us if the transplant was successful."

"It's just too soon to know, my dears," she said. "It takes hours, even days, until we will know if Shevi's body is accepting the new kidney." She drew in a deep breath and took another sip of coffee.

"Mommy...will you stay with Shevi in the hospital tonight...seder night?" asked Esther sadly.

"Let me, Mommy. I could sleep there tonight and stay with Shevi all day tomorrow," I pleaded.

"Thank you, Yehudis," Mommy answered. "But I have to be there. Tonight will be critical." There was a decided tremor in her voice. Esther and I had often relieved Mommy at Shevi's bedside in the hospital, both in the daytime and at night. But now Mommy was so tense, not her usual calm self at all, so I let it go. We all understood her fear that maybe, God forbid, it had all been for nothing.

"I hope you understand, Yehudis," Mommy said. "I know you'd all like me to be here with you for the seder. I'd like to be here, too." Her voice broke and a few tears slid down her cheeks. "But I just couldn't bear to sit here and enjoy our seder while my little girl is lying in the ward in pain, when I still don't know how she is, whether she'll reject the transplant or not." A few more tears fell, and Mommy had to get up and hurry out of the room. "Let her just live...let her just live...."

We hadn't realized until now that Shevi's life was in danger. The steady ticking of the wall clock accompanied our silent prayers like the rhythm of the *U'Nesaneh Tokef* prayer we say on Rosh HaShanah: "Who shall live...and who shall die...." We hadn't known that if the body rejects a transplant, the results can sometimes be tragic.

We echoed Mommy's prayer, each in his own words: "Just let her live." "Please, Hashem, let her live and be well." "Send a *refuah sheleimah* to Batsheva bas Henya."

On the seder night, when Jews all over the world were at home, sitting around tables set with the finest utensils, gleaming glass goblets, and fine china dishes, reading from beautifully illustrated Haggados, regally leaning on cushions, on this most spiritually meaningful night, a woman sat in Hadassah Hospital beside a girl — her daughter— who lay in bed attached to a myriad of tubes.

"Shevi," Mommy said gently.

"Yes, Mommy?"

"Let's make our own seder, here, together. Would you like to?"

Shevi lay on her bed, drifting in and out of sleep. Mommy poured a glass of wine and recited the Kiddush. "Now, Shevi, I'll recite the *Mah Nishtanah* for you...." Very quietly, Mommy began to chant the Four Questions traditionally asked by children at the seder. Smiling, Shevi fell asleep.

Mommy sang a few more songs from the Haggadah and sat there contemplating her sleeping daughter.

"Mommy." Shevi opened her eyes groggily and asked, "What were you just singing to me? It was a beautiful melody."

"Try to remember, Shevi," Mommy encouraged her.

"Uh...was it *Avadim Hayinu*? Or maybe *Vehi She'amdah*?" Again, Shevi drifted off. She was unable to stay awake for more than a minute or two.

An hour passed; Mommy continued reading to herself from the Haggadah. Suddenly Shevi groaned aloud. "Mommy, it hurts...."

Mommy stroked Shevi's cheek, smoothed her wispy hair. "Soon they'll bring you something to ease the pain. Shevi, I've hidden the *afikoman*, can you guess where? If you guess, you get a present; if you don't, I get one!"

"All right, Mommy, I'll try. Is it...in the cabinet next to my bed?"

"No."

"Is it in your blue carryall?"

"No."

"Is it...." Shevi was asleep again.

"*Avadim hayinu* — We were slaves in bondage.... Please, Hashem, free Shevi from her bondage! From being a slave to dialysis!" She remembered how Shevi looked when she was attached to the dialysis machine. She thought about all those children who were attached — enslaved — each to their own machine, and she shuddered. She raised her eyes and tearfully prayed, "Please, Hashem, set her free from those treatments!"

Now, a pause was called for in the Haggadah. It was time to have the festive meal. Mommy had brought small plastic containers of food with her for her feast. She tasted some of the fish, then some of the cooked chicken, but she had a large lump of choked-back tears in her throat that checked her appetite. She thought about the family at home, about her other children, and wondered how their seder was proceeding.

She thought of little Moishy, her only son, who was so mature for his age, so understanding. Would he always remember his mother in terms of running off to hospitals and doctors? Well, there really wasn't much she could do about it. The main thing right now was for Shevi's condition to improve.

"Mommy..." Shevi sighed. She was such a tiny figure, lost among the white sheets in the large bed.

"Have you guessed yet, Shevi?"

But Shevi's eyes closed again. It was almost midnight, time to eat the *afikoman*, the first half of the second matzah. Shevi awoke again.

"I've just eaten the *afikoman*, Shevi. You owe me a present." Mommy smiled.

Shevi's answering smile was forced; she could barely speak. "Mommy," she said, turning her enormous, pain-filled eyes toward her mother, "yes, you deserve a present. But not just an *afikoman* present. You deserve a really special present, a great big giant of a present...for being such a wonderful mother. A mother who has seen me through...so much, who has given me such support and always kept my spirits up...." And Shevi slept, this time with the trace of a smile on her lips, a smile of recognition for a very special mother who had walked beside her, hand in hand, with patience and tenderness, sharing her courage and faith with her tormented daughter.

The room was quiet except for Shevi's occasional moans of pain. Mommy was awed at what Shevi had just said. At such a time, to thank her mother! "*Ribbono shel Olam,*" she murmured, "Thank You for giving me such a precious little girl! This child is a living *mussar sefer* for all of us! Thank You!"

While Mommy and Shevi were wrapped in the poignant silence of the hospital room, we at home were doing our best to make our seder night as pleasant and cheerful as we could. The table was beautifully set with our best dishes and silverware on a sparkling white tablecloth; a bouquet of flowers in a vase sweetly scented the air.

You might think that we were feeling forsaken and forlorn. Not at all! Abba sat at the head of the table, smiling and cheerful, reclining on his pillow as a noble and free man ought to. Scattered among us were a few invited guests who had no seder of their own. Although Mommy had tried to dissuade Abba from inviting guests since she wouldn't be with us, Abba would not forego this mitzvah.

"Guests are the best *segulah* for Shevi," Abba told her, his clear blue eyes shining with determination. "Having guests for the *seder* will be the most important thing we can do for Shevi — mitzvos, only mitzvos will plead our cause above."

CHAPTER TWENTY-ONE

OH, BANANAS!

❧ ❧

N aturally, the very minute the holiday was over, Mommy called. Bashi picked up the telephone.

"How is Shevi? Is everything all right? Is the kidney being accepted? When can we visit?"

"How about letting Mommy talk?" Grandma said. "How can she tell you anything if you don't wait for any answers?"

Bashi handed the telephone to Grandma and we all listened in suspenseful silence. We couldn't really tell from her expression whether the news was good or bad, but she soon calmed our fears.

"The operation itself was successful, *baruch Hashem*," Savta said, "but it will take a few days to know if the kidney is being accepted."

The next afternoon, Tovah Leah, Bashi, and I walked along the rose-bordered path leading to the hospital entrance. It was a beautiful spring day and we were on vacation from school for the entire week of Pesach. The sun was shining and the sky was such a clear, rich blue that you felt you could reach up and touch it. We were on our way to visit Shevi and we were tense with expectation and fear. The failure of her first transplant operation was still fresh in our minds — the sound of her bitter cry of disappointment still echoed in our ears. The memory of it made us tremble, and not only were we fearful that the tragic scene would repeat itself, but we also didn't want to see Shevi disappointed yet again.

Our hearts were heavy with apprehension as we rode to the eighth floor in an elevator packed with other silent, serious-faced visitors.

We entered the ward and slowly approached room number eight. I can't remember which one of us murmured, "With Hashem's help, it will be good."

And there was Shevi, lying in bed...and her face, her face was not yellow anymore. It was a healthy-looking pink color! We couldn't believe our eyes. The last time we had seen her, in fact for as long as we could remember, her skin had been a sickly yellowish-white. She always used to pinch her cheeks when she looked in the mirror, to get a little bit of color in them. We'd offer facetiously to give her a slap and she would insist she didn't mind it at all, if it would help.

"Shevi!" Bashi rushed over to kiss her. "You're pink!"

"I know," she answered with a grin. "I can't believe it either. I asked Mommy to bring me a mirror so I could see it for myself!" There was a happy lilt in her voice and a gleam of satisfaction in her eyes.

Mommy came in then with a mirror she had just purchased downstairs in the gift shop and gave it to Shevi. We watched her raising it to her face and complacently looking at herself.

"Mommy, why didn't you tell us?" I asked.

"I asked her not to," said Shevi. "I wanted to see if you'd notice by yourselves. I wanted to see your reaction."

What a small, ordinary thing it is to have healthy, normal, pink-tinged skin. But how often do we ever stop to think about it or appreciate that we have it!

"The only candy we could bring this time, Shevi, is kosher-for-Pesach Swiss chocolate bars," Tovah Leah told her.

"That's wonderful!" Shevi smiled brightly at us.

In walked a smiling doctor. "Hello there, Shevi. How are you feeling?" As he reached for her wrist to check her pulse, he spied a basket of fruit standing on the bedside cabinet. "Well,

Shevi, how would you like to eat one of these bananas? I'm sure you like them, don't you?"

Shevi's smile froze. She looked at the smiling doctor, at the tantalizing bananas, and back at the doctor. She hadn't been able to eat a banana for years because of its high potassium content.

"Go ahead, take one," he said. "You're not a dialysis patient anymore. You can eat all the bananas in the basket if you like!"

We sat in silence for a few moments, absorbing what the doctor had said. Then Bashi grabbed Shevi's hand and shook it. "*Mazal tov, mazal tov,*" she exclaimed. "You are no longer a dialysis patient!"

"What beautiful words," Shevi said. "Say them again, please!"

Looking very pleased, the doctor patted her shoulder, said he'd come in again later, and walked out. Our smiles of joy competed with the bright sunshine that streamed in through the windows. We felt that the whole world was smiling. We laughed and chattered and watched with great empathy as Shevi ate her first banana.

Nurses and doctors heard our gay laughter and peeked in to see what was causing all the commotion. They, too, smiled with understanding and pleasure.

Suddenly, Shevi stopped smiling and looked at us mournfully.

"Whatever is the matter, Shevi? Are you in pain?" we asked.

"Of course I'm in pain," she said, "but that's not what's bothering me. I know I have to suffer in order to be healthy again, to grow taller, to be free from dialysis. But that's a wonderful kind of pain."

We were at a loss to understand her sudden, drastic change of mood and couldn't fathom what she meant.

"It hurts me to think of my neighbor in the next room. I just saw her son pass by; he's going in to visit her. What could be worse than a son having to visit such a sick mother?" Shevi's eyes filled with tears. "Ilana's kidneys aren't working, and neither is her pancreas. Her body rejected the transplant, and her condition is serious; she looks awful.

"It's hard for me to be happy," she continued, "when I think of Ilana. She has five children. I keep thinking: I wish I could transfer some of my success to her. Her children need her; they need a healthy mother, and I...."

We were shocked. Shevi felt guilty!

"But we need you, Shevi. And Mommy can't live without you. You are her most beloved daughter!"

Our ardent response surprised Shevi. She never thought of herself as special, and was always humbly astonished to receive praise. Moreover, she had always been extremely reticent and reluctant to reveal her emotions to anyone. We could see she was moved, and we could only hope her restored health would make her more relaxed and open with us.

"Thank you for saying that," she replied. "But even though it's nice to hear that, I still feel awful about Ilana. Whenever I see one of her children come to visit her, I feel so bad. A nurse told me they might move her in here tomorrow — oh, I hope they will!"

We were taken aback. Why would they do that? It seemed to us that having such a roommate might set Shevi's condition back, and we were strongly tempted to intervene and ask the nurses not to do such a thing to Shevi.

Shevi apparently sensed our feelings and hastened to assure us that she really would be happy to have Ilana in the room with her. She began to enumerate all the ways she might help her, even though she was so much younger. She could tell her how disappointed she had been when the first transplant was rejected; she could encourage her children to be hopeful and have courage. Who knew how much she might help?

"You know," she said thoughtfully, "perhaps it was a good

thing that my first transplant was not successful. Maybe Hashem intended it so that now I can encourage others by telling them not to give up, not to despair...."

It was an extraordinary thing to witness. Here lay Shevi, weak and in pain a few days after a delicate, dangerous operation. Her coloring had only just begun to look normal, yet she paid no attention to her own problems. She ignored the fact that she herself was only at the beginning of the long road to recovery, that it was still uncertain how long her body would accept its new kidney. It wasn't even definite that her growth potential would be improved, that she would cease to be a small person. Yet not a word did we hear about her own worries or feelings; she was only concerned for the unfortunate woman in the next room and how she herself could help.

CHAPTER TWENTY-TWO

THANK YOU, SHEVI!

ε& ε&

*T*he woman in the next bed looked terrible; her skin was yellow, she was very thin, and she was hooked up to several machines. The instant she saw Mother and me walk into the hospital room, she said, "Shevi is such a wonderful girl; she is really amazing."

Shevi tried to stop the flow of compliments, but the woman continued praising her with shining eyes. "She helps me so much. She is so encouraging, and she knows just how to lift my spirits." Ilana's face belied her words, however. She smiled at us, but she looked weary and seemed to be in great pain.

"I don't know how much longer I have to live," she said, "but Shevi gives me courage."

A pretty, dark-eyed, ten-year-old girl sat next to Ilana, stroking her hand. "Don't try to talk, Ima," she said. "It tires you, and you have to rest; you have to get better."

"Oh, Sarit! What a precious child the Creator has blessed me with. What wonderful children I've been granted." She squeezed Sarit's hand weakly and drifted off to sleep. Sarit looked at her mother's face and tears filled her eyes.

"It will be all right, Sarit," said Mommy softly. "With Hashem's help, she'll get better."

"I...don't think so," the girl whispered woefully. "She just keeps getting weaker from day to day. You see, my brother is to be married next week. He's the oldest, and Ima was so happy when he became engaged. She was so looking forward to seeing all her children happily married. She's such a wonderful mother. Even when she is so sick, she always tries so hard to take care of us." Sarit sniffed and wiped away some of her tears with the back of her hand.

"I don't even know if Ima will be able to be at his wedding. We don't know what her condition will be next week...."

Shevi's compassion was awakened by the child's despair. "You know, Sarit," she said a bit bashfully, "there were times when they thought I wouldn't live...." She looked at Mommy for confirmation and Mommy nodded her head.

"Many years ago, my mother and father were planning to go to England to consult with a big specialist there. He was a friend of the family and they were sure they would get the best help possible from him. They were ready to take me with them, too. But when they spoke on the telephone he said that he had enough information from the reports they had sent him. He told them...."

Sarit was listening closely, her tears held back for the moment.

"...according to the medical data he'd seen, he and his colleagues were sure that I had only a few more months to live!" Shevi smiled at Sarit. "Do you see? Things looked really black, but Hashem is good and He wanted things to be otherwise. He wanted to give me a task to perform in His world."

Shevi sighed deeply. "Do you see the color of my face? Do you know what it means? I never dreamed a week ago that I'd look healthy, or that I would be eating bananas freely, and so many other things that I was not allowed to have for such a long time.

"We just have to pray, we have to have faith. Despair is not allowed; we can't let ourselves get depressed. We just have to pray, and pray, and pray."

Sarit was still sitting quietly next to her mother's bed a few hours later when the nurses came around to check the patients. The red-haired nurse removed the thermometer from Shevi's mouth and her eyes widened. She quickly took a second thermometer from the tray and asked Shevi to let her try again. As the nurse put the second thermometer into her mouth, Shevi felt a wave of dizziness pass over her, but she sat quietly in the bed, looking at the nurse's mop of red hair and trying to interpret the frown of concern on her forehead.

"I'm sorry, dear, but you have a fever. I'm going to call the doctor."

Shevi stretched out her hand to the siddur on her bedside cabinet. When she opened it, the letters swam before her eyes and danced a weird jig. The book slipped from her fingers, and she lay back on the pillow. She felt sick and very, very warm.

Sarit stood up in alarm and asked Shevi what the matter was. When she saw that Shevi couldn't answer her, she ran out into the hall to call the first nurse she saw.

A short, chubby nurse stopped in her tracks and hurried into the room. She put her hand on Shevi's forehead; Shevi was tossing around in the bed and seemed to be having difficulty breathing.

"All right, Shevi, try to lie quietly." A second nurse rushed in, and was told to get Dr. Sender immediately. The chubby nurse brought Shevi a glass of water and tried to get her to sip some. Shevi did not look at all well. Her cheeks were painted with an unhealthy flush and she was moving restlessly about. Sarit stood by tensely.

"What's going on?" Mommy entered the room. She took in the scene at a glance and turned pale. "It isn't another rejection, is it?"

"Let's hope not," said the nurse.

Dr. Sender rushed in. He examined Shevi briskly but thoroughly and said, "It looks like she has an infection somewhere. I will start her on antibiotics immediately, even though I can't localize it at this point." He hurriedly wrote out some instructions and gave them to the nurse.

Soon the red-haired nurse came back with a plastic bag in her hands which she hooked up to the intravenous apparatus and attached it to the needle still in Shevi's hand.

"Why the intravenous?" Mommy asked.

"She needs a very strong antibiotic and she needs it in large doses, too large to administer orally."

Mommy sank down on a chair next to Shevi's bed and started to pray. "Hashem, please let this end well; let me see her recovered and able to come home!"

"What's going to happen to Shevi?" asked Sarit hesitantly, holding on tightly to her sleeping mother's hand.

"Don't worry," Mommy answered firmly. "Hashem will help. Shevi was so happy...it can't be that her happiness was for nothing. I never saw Shevi become excited about her recuperation before. No, it cannot be that she'll be disappointed this time." Mommy's voice faltered. "She has gone through so much, and it has always been she who encourages the rest of us, who calms and comforts everyone around her...."

Sarit burst into tears.

"Why are you crying, Sarit?" Mommy asked.

"How can you ask?" Sarit sobbed. "I can't stand to see Shevi suffering again...and she has encouraged me so much the last few days."

Mommy went over and hugged the brave little girl. "You'll see. With Hashem's help, everything will be fine. I think this is just a small infection. You know, after a transplant, the patient is susceptible to any passing germ. A few days of antibiotics and, with the help of God, Shevi will be well again."

Sarit managed a tiny smile. "Shevi just has to get well. I couldn't stand it to see her disappointed a second time. Besides..." She looked from her sleeping mother to Shevi and back to Mommy. "...I don't think her job is over yet. I...I'm going to need her...I'm going to need her strength and comfort. Ima's condition is getting critical. I need to hear Shevi's optimistic words. I have a feeling that...my mother is not going to get better and...I'll need to hear Shevi's soothing words even more...."

Shevi was still burning with fever three days later — three stressful days.

"I think we'll have to change the antibiotic," Dr. Sender said with concern. When that didn't seem to make a difference either, Mommy and Abba decided to call the transplant center in Boston and ask whether this fever was a normal phenomenon after a transplant or not. The doctors in Boston assured them that this was a fairly common reaction, and that they would prescribe the same course of antibiotics — it was a matter of time.

Shevi lay with cool compresses on her forehead. She could barely answer questions put to her, and the fever remained high. Yet, whenever she could summon enough energy, she turned to Sarit to ask how the little girl was and how her mother was faring.

Sarit went to stand next to Shevi. She couldn't believe Shevi had the strength to worry about someone else.

"What does strength have to do with it?" Shevi asked. "I think about...you and your mother...all the time. You are such a nice girl, and you have such a...wonderful mother. I pray for you both...that Hashem give you the will to...accept...."

"To accept...." Sarit was afraid to finish the sentence.

Shevi struggled to raise herself up part-way. She hugged Sarit warmly with one arm, though the arm shook from the fever, and said, "Hashem will help."

Sarit released all the tears and tension she had been holding back for so many weeks, and wept in Shevi's arms. The facade of a mature, responsible young woman, trying to keep things together for her siblings and be brave before her mother, crumbled in an instant and she reverted to the ten-year-old she was.

"Cry, Sarit! Cry! It's good for you...to let go.... It will help you so that you can be strong."

Soon the flood of tears abated. "I feel better now," Sarit whispered tremulously. "Do you know, I have felt a lump in my throat for such a long time, but it's gone now. I hope...I think...maybe I'll be able to cope...to encourage and strengthen my father and my sisters, and my mother.... Thank you, Shevi!"

CHAPTER TWENTY-THREE

CHUPPAH IN ROOM EIGHT

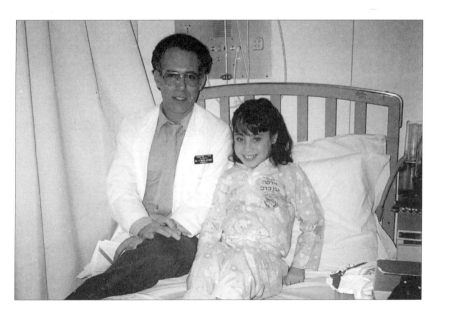

ba ba

*I*lana opened her eyes slowly and looked around the hospital
room. Beribboned balloons festooned the walls and hung
from the ceiling. A banner reading *"Mazal Tov!"* ran across the
windows. The sun's rays picked out the bright colors of the dec-
orations, the pristine whiteness of the sheets draped across the
two thin figures lying in the two beds, and the irridescent blue
party dress on the young girl seated between them.

"This is a fine wedding hall, Ilana," Shevi said with enthusiasm. "How fortunate that you are Sephardim and can have the
chuppah indoors." Shevi had, thank God, recovered from the
frightening infection and was recuperating from the transplant
operation.

"You're right about one thing," murmured Ilana. "My son's
wedding is being held in a most unusual hall...but at least I'll be
at the ceremony, *b'ezras Hashem!*"

"Ima, let me fix your pillows so you can sit up," said Sarit,
arranging the bedding for her mother. "They'll be here soon."

A *chuppah* in a hospital room: a moment of great emotion
— and great sadness.

Ilana's sister Shula was the first to arrive, dressed in shiny
black silk dress studded with rhinestones, with a tape player under her arm. She set the player down on the bedside cabinet and
pressed a button, and cheerful wedding music filled the air.
Ilana looked at her older sister, then gazed out the window at
the trees beyond. She saw the golden oranges sheltered among

the deep green of the branches. Who would shelter her "fruit" in the days and years to come? she wondered sorrowfully.

"*Mazal tov*, Ilana!" Shula bent over her sister and kissed her fondly. With an effort, Ilana banished her melancholy thoughts and smiled back.

One after another, the immediate family of the bride and groom arrived, trying to mask their distress with a festive manner and cheerful greetings. A sister-in-law shook Ilana's frail hand, saying, "*Mazal tov*! May you merit to see many more celebrations."

"May it only be so," Ilana murmured.

The bride arrived to the accompaniment of the traditional wedding melody sung by her family as they entered the room. Clad modestly in a white, lacy gown and smiling shyly, she was seated in a flower-bedecked armchair placed next to Ilana's bed.

Ilana put out a trembling hand and grasped the bride's hand, holding on for several minutes with tears running down her cheeks. How she wanted to hold on to the moment! How she wanted to live long enough to spend time with her daughter-in-law and enjoy having the young couple as guests in her home!

"Racheli," she said to the lovely bride. "Take good care of my son...be a good wife to him...." Tears choked off her words.

The bride, deeply moved, also began to cry. She understood the solemnity of the moment, that her soon-to-be husband was the eldest child and she herself might soon be called upon to be a mother to her young brothers- and sisters-in-law.

Both families stood still and watched the pale, sick woman attached to an intravenous tube and the beautiful young woman embracing her.

Sarit, dressed in a long, blue gown with her dark hair artfully arranged, reached over and rearranged her mother's pillows once more to make her as comfortable as possible. Ilana smiled her thanks.

They heard the chanting of a wedding tune and the groom appeared in the doorway, accompanied by his father and the bride's father, one on either side. The bride sat in her chair, head lowered, praying. Tall and handsome, his face reflecting the momentous nature of the occasion, the groom slowly walked toward his bride. As he bent forward to draw the veil over her face in the traditional manner, every face in the room was wet with tears.

He turned to his mother. "Ima," he said softly, "give me your blessing."

Ilana looked up at him through tear-filled eyes. This was her firstborn; she could still see the smiling, chubby infant he had been twenty-two years before. How could she have imagined she would be seeing him to the *chuppah* from a hospital bed, under such circumstances?

"My son," she whispered earnestly. "May you merit to have great happiness...in good health...all the days of your life. May you merit seeing joy from your descendants...."

The chanting continued. The groom was led to the canopy held up by four tall, male cousins. Now Ilana and the bride's mother were to escort the bride to the canopy. Her sisters helped the patient stand up and walk with the bride; one of the women pushed along the intravenous stand behind Ilana. Everyone cried, some sobbed aloud.

Shevi took Sarit's hand and walked with her, slowly, behind Ilana. They too were crying. Terrible thoughts numbed Sarit; she was so afraid her mother hadn't long to live. Why, tomorrow she might be an orphan! Shevi put a thin arm around her and whispered, "Pray, Sarit! These are sacred moments. When a bride and groom are united under their wedding canopy, Hashem is near. Ask Him to grant your wishes."

Sarit took the tissues Shevi held out, wiped her tears, and prayed, "Please, Hashem, send good health and recovery to my mother...." Her tears flowed anew.

The blessings were being pronounced. Everyone listened raptly in order to answer each blessing with a heartfelt "Amen!"

The bridegroom stamped on the glass and shattered it in memory of the destruction of the Temple. The exaltation felt in that hospital room was palpable.

"*Mazal tov!*" Kisses, hugs, and blessings were exchanged freely, great joy temporarily banishing the tears.

"*Mazal tov*, my son," Ilana said, feeling the room begin to spin around her. "Be strong," she told herself, "for just a few more minutes. Don't let anyone realize how weak you are!"

"It's time to go to the wedding hall for the meal now," Shevi told Sarit urgently. Her sharp eyes noticed Ilana holding on tightly to her sister's arm. She turned to Aunt Shula and whispered shyly, "I think you should hurry them up now and leave on a happy note. Ilana needs to rest."

Aunt Shula understood the message and with an authoritative air, hustled everyone out with more wishes of "*Mazal tov! Mazal tov!*"

Shevi walked a little way with Sarit to encourage her. "Dance at the wedding, Sarit.... Be happy!"

Sarit gave Shevi a kiss and hurried to catch up with her family. Shevi looked after her with a grim smile. *If only*, she thought, *she merits having her mother a while longer. Oh, Hashem! Please send a refuah sheleimah to Ilana bas Perachya,* she prayed from the bottom of her heart.

Shevi submerged her own pain and suffering in total absorption and concern for Sarit and Ilana. All her prayers and wishes were for a speedy recovery for Ilana.

CHAPTER TWENTY-FOUR

A MEMORABLE TEACHER

&❧ &❧

*P*urim was in the air. Shevi had returned to school and joined
her classmates moving up to high school, participating fully
in every class and in every activity. There were two weeks left before the holiday and the girls were buzzing with excitement. In
addition to the Purim Fair that the senior classes prepared, each
of the lower classes planned their own celebration.

Shevi's teacher announced that they would have a lottery
for the exchange of *mishloach manos* among the girls at the class
Purim party. She placed a cardboard shoebox on her desk containing slips of colored paper; each slip bore the name of one of
the girls. They would file up one by one and draw a name from
the box. The results would of course be kept secret, and each girl
was expected to prepare a package that would somehow be appropriate for the recipient, something that would reflect that
girl's special talents or character.

I noticed that Shevi was particularly nervous and tense.
When I asked her what was bothering her, she told me about the
lottery. She had somehow found out that the teacher herself
had drawn her name and was preparing Shevi's Purim package.

"How on earth do you know that?" I asked.

"Well, everyone has been talking and snooping and com-
paring notes and, you know, they've somehow figured it out."

"So why are you worried? The girls are all probably jealous
of you!"

"Yes, but...."

"But what? What is there to be worried about?"

"Well, because...what can the teacher possibly find special about me...to mention...other than my height?" she finally blurted out.

"Now you're being ridiculous!" I told her sharply. "You have so many good qualities and special traits."

"Yehudis, don't be angry," Shevi pleaded. "I'm just so on edge."

I looked at Shevi with concern. Frail, delicate little Shevi. What indeed would the teacher find to emphasize about her? Would her teacher realize how many wonderful qualities she had? Had she noticed that Shevi was just like any other girl her age, with many interests and sensitivities? Now I was worried, too.

As the days passed, Mommy and I waited tensely along with Shevi to see what "package" her teacher would deem suitable. Would it be complimentary, or would Shevi be insulted by too faint praise? We all felt extremely protective toward Shevi and didn't want to see her hurt.

On the day of the Purim parties, Tovah Leah, Bashi, and I arrived home from school before Shevi. We had no patience to do anything other than sit and wait for her. We joined Mommy in the kitchen and had something to drink, jumping at each sound we heard. Once it was a neighbor carrying several shopping baskets who made a lot of noise getting out of the elevator; once it was a man selling sheepskin rugs. Surely the party must be over by now. What was keeping her?

Suddenly, quietly, the door opened and there she was! Her arms were full, her eyes were shining, her face was lit with happiness and joy. She even seemed to us to have grown taller!

"Shevi! How was the party?" we chorused.

"It was just wonderful!" she sang out, putting down her packages of sweets and holding out a booklet for our inspection.

The booklet contained six sheets of colored paper, stapled together and decorated with ribbons; on each page were photographs of Shevi, from infancy to the present, with a written description under each one telling something about her.

The following is the poem the teacher wrote:

To Shevi,
We're not talking about any old someone,
But a special, multi-faceted personality!
From the minute this twin was born,
Shevi was already making history!
A matching set: Shevi and Bashi,
With matching green, ever-smiling eyes.
Eyes that are always content and sharing
Their friends' joys and sighs.

And something else about those eyes:
(It will not come as a surprise
To those who understand kids of this tender age)
Shevi's eyes already showed
A future talent for the stage.
In short, an energetic pair,
They see that all is good;
An example through all life's trials and stresses.
'Tis not easy to be optimistic as we should.

Though others may bear the name Shevi,
None can compare to such a degree
With our Shevi, so gracious and clever;
I'm sure you will all agree.
If you saw Shevi performing on the stage,
Her talent noticed from an early age,
You'd see great wisdom in her eyes,
And warmth and something playful.

No, it's no surprise
That her natural, unaffected manner
Conquered audiences near and far;
And in the top roles that she's played,
Shevi has always been a star!

Now we've proved that Shevi's great,
We'll predict even greater fame.
We'll tell of Shevi's travels, just you wait;
Wherever she's been she has a good name.

To America, to France, and of course, Israel,
To California, Pennsylvania, and Colorado,
To Denver, to Paris,
Who knows where Shevi will yet go?
So many different scenes,
And Shevi's only in her teens!

Sometimes she talks,
And sometimes she's still.
Because not everything that she's thinking
Does she have to spill.
Yet she has much to say
In her own special way.

Shevi's a skillful seamstress, too.
And when she sews something new,
It's never ordinary, as you can see;
For there's nothing ordinary about Shevi.

Right now, for instance, she's having lots of fun
Sewing a new blazer; it's almost done.
And this fits in, it's all one chain
Of taste, talent, imagination, and lots of *chein*.

One more surprise, and it is this, no less:
Shevi is also a poetess.
And if in another ten or twenty years,
You find a book of poetry moving you to tears,
It simply must be Shevi's, who started her career
Writing letters of her experiences there and here.

Though life is sometimes happy, sometimes sad,
'Tis always an adventure, and that's not bad.
Shevi has a lot to tell,
And she will tell it very well.

She'll write about what's happy and what's less
With humor, satire, skill, and finesse.
And just look at her letters, her handwriting, too;
Graphics is something else that she can do!

Well, it's time to sign off now.
But first, to Shevi's sisters: Take a bow!
Bashi is always at Shevi's side,
With patience and kindness she cannot hide.

Bashi shares her sister's every moan
And rejoices in her joy as in her own.
Indeed, there's much to write of Bashi,
It's just that now the topic's Shevi!

One more *yasher koach* and we'll be done:
To Yehudis, a great sister, in more ways than one!

To Shevi, in the name of all the class,
It remains only to say:
Our sister! May you be for thousands

And for tens of thousands! And may
You climb higher, ever higher,
Succeeding always, in every way!

From your class

We read the poem with great emotion, filled with wonder at this sensitive, caring teacher who had taken the trouble to get to know Shevi and appreciate all her good qualities. I cannot fully express our feeling of gratitude to her, and Shevi's happiness on that occasion is indescribable.

The tribute in that booklet showed us why that was Shevi's most precious year in high school; why Shevi bloomed that year. It is undeniable that a person can sense when he is appreciated, when others care, and this sweet feeling did wonders for Shevi.

Moreover, this was a further lesson to us, if we hadn't already learned it, of the power an individual possesses to influence others. One can, if he chooses, raise others up or dash them down; he can help others to feel self-worth and dignity or, Heaven forbid, worthless and despised. Oh, how careful each one of us must always be not to tread on someone's soul!

CHAPTER TWENTY-FIVE

INTERIOR DECORATING

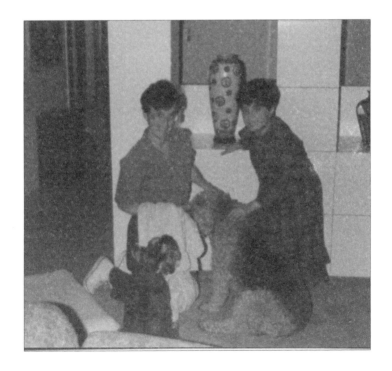

એક એક

*C*hedva and Ziva, friends of ours who lived in the same building, stood just inside our front door and looked around in awe. Shevi laughed at their astonishment and said agreeably, "Yes, it is a pretty weird way to decorate the house."

Chedva read aloud from the posters hung on every side: "Active voice, past tense. First person — *halachti* (I went); second person — *halachta* (you went); third person...."

Ziva continued, "And here's the passive voice." A smile of comprehension dimpled her cheeks. "This is super, Shevi!"

The walls of almost every room in our apartment, plus the hallways, were hung, not with drawings or embroidered pictures, but with charts and lists of Hebrew grammar! Yellow, pink, and blue posters, with conjugations of verbs neatly printed in large letters: yellow was active voice; pink was reflexive voice; blue was passive voice. White ones hung between the colored ones to denote exceptions to the rules. Our whole apartment was "studying" for the grammar exam.

It had all started when Shevi and Bashi had come home from school one day looking worried. We were, as usual, sitting around our wide kitchen table eating supper, and they joined us.

"You know," said Shevi, "we've got final exams in two weeks. I don't think I can take the grammar exam."

"Why not?" we asked.

"I don't even know the basic rules of conjugation, much

less the difference between the active and passive voices," she complained.

"If you don't have strength to go through it..." Mommy hastened to reassure her. When she saw Tovah Leah and me glaring, she added defensively, "Well, grammar is a very difficult subject!"

"Sure it's difficult," I said. "But Shevi can do it!"

"This time, I...I really don't think so." Shevi fixed despairing eyes on us.

I kept silent because I didn't want to start a whole discussion in front of Mommy. I knew it was hard for her to encourage Shevi to study harder. Mommy had been at the hospital with her so often and sat with her through hours of painful and debilitating treatments, hours of suffering, nausea, and dizziness. She knew Shevi's medical condition better than I. Besides, it wasn't logically possible for Shevi to get a grade of more than thirty percent on an examination, for she had only been present in class thirty percent of the time.

Shevi had been missing classes for years. She had undergone so many operations we had lost count. A burst vein was a matter of routine for her, and she needed weekly blood tests. How could she possibly sit down and study after a day of grueling, physically exhausting treatment? All the girls in her class were feeling stress before this exam, and they had been present, they had listened to the teacher's explanations, they'd all had time to study for hours in the afternoons and evenings in order to pass.

I remembered the many hours I had studied for this exam; I recalled how tense my friends and I had been. I knew that my sister Tovah Leah, an excellent student, the best in her class, had needed many hours to prepare for it in her time. I was wary of encouraging Shevi to try, and I just couldn't decide what to do. Would it be so terrible if she missed one exam?

We finished supper and I was still undecided. I went into

my room to read, but the letters blurred before my eyes. Doubt gnawed at me. Why should I encourage her to work so hard and make herself sicker, all to no purpose? On the other hand, if she didn't take the exam she'd be miserable and disappointed in herself, feeling left out of things again. I went so far as to picture her reaction when all her friends would be busy discussing the exam with each other and asking each other for examples and exceptions and rules and punctuation and Shevi would not be able to say a word. I envisioned them turning to her and asking if she had already finished studying and was prepared already. I could see the flush that would spread over her face and hear her tell them in embarassment that she wasn't going to take the exam. Her friends would be astonished, and Shevi would feel terrible.

"No!" I said, bounding out of my chair. "It won't do! Shevi has got to be included in everything. She has to be able to feel like everyone else." I could not let Shevi succumb; I would have to help her overcome the obstacles. Of course, it would be a double battle; first, to persuade Mommy that Shevi could and should do it, and second, to figure out how to do it.

I wandered about the apartment, deep in thought. She could do it; I knew she could! She had the brain power and the willpower. In my determination for her to succeed, I had clenched my fists without realizing it.

"Why do you look so fierce?" Shevi asked me. "You look like you're ready to do battle!" Her enormous, sad eyes searched mine.

For a moment, I didn't know what to say.

"Tell me," she urged. "What's the matter?"

"Shevi," I said, weighing my words, "I was thinking about your grammar exam. I think you should take it, and I think you're going to pass it!"

She was astonished to hear my words. "Do you...really think I have a chance?"

"I don't think so, I know it!"

"But how?" she asked doubtfully. "You know the whole story. I'm absent more often than not absent; I don't even know the basic rules, much less all the details of conjugations and endings and voices; I don't even know where to begin to study for such an exam."

We talked about it at length. We identified her weak points and discussed the general outline of the work to be covered. Then we hit upon the idea of making wall charts. I told her it wouldn't be easy, far from it — she would have to invest hours of study even with the visual aids we dreamed up. Shevi assured me that she was ready to try. She was determined to do whatever was necessary to be like her friends, to keep up with everything they did.

That same day we went out to buy several giant sheets of construction paper in various colors, a box of colored markers, and plenty of Scotch tape.

Shevi was soon at work at the dining room table. She made her charts and posters and lists following the rules in the grammar textbook. All the voices, all the conjugations, all the persons came under her scrutiny and were soon marching in order up and down the sheets of colored paper. Occasionally she would ask us for some help before she wrote out a section and pasted it up on the wall.

Shevi smiled at Mommy, her eyes shining with enthusiasm. "I already feel better," she said. "Every time I go past, I read a list and say it over to myself. Now I really feel I'm getting into it; before, it was all a closed book to me."

Mommy just nodded and shrugged her shoulders; she was happy to see Shevi pleased, but she was still afraid that, despite her efforts, it would just be too much for her and in the end she'd fail.

"You know, Yehudis," Shevi said to me at one point, "even if I fail...well, I'll be very upset, of course, but I still won't be sorry I made the effort. At least I'm finally catching up with everyone in grammar. In a day or two, I'll be just like the rest of the class." This was so important to her. "At least in grammar, I won't feel so...small!"

I gave her a huge hug and told her I had a feeling she would pass the test with a good mark. Where did my confidence come from? I'm not sure. Perhaps it was seeing the determination in her eyes, perhaps it was knowing how intelligent she was, how strong her willpower was. In any case, I felt I knew her better than anyone else and I was convinced she would succeed, for if she failed — I didn't know who would feel worse. I didn't permit myself to imagine her failing.

One evening while Shevi was walking about the house memorizing the rules of Hebrew grammar, there was a knock at the door. One of Shevi's friends, Efrat, had come to see her. Shevi was concentrating so hard on one of her wall charts that she didn't even hear Efrat speak to her. Tall, blond Efrat walked over and tapped her on the shoulder.

Shevi was startled. "Oh! Hello, Efrat. I'm sorry I didn't hear you come in. I was so wrapped up in this grammar."

"Yes, I know," Efrat replied. "As a matter of fact, that's why I came. I'm missing several exceptions to some of the rules, and I...um...don't really have the patience to start looking them all up by myself." She smiled shyly at Shevi. "So I thought...um...maybe I could come and study from your lists." She looked around the room in wonder. "I've never seen anything like this. It's all so clear! Do you mind?"

"Of course not," Shevi said. "I'm happy that for once I can contribute something and not always be on the receiving end."

Efrat went from chart to chart, from wall to wall, and read off the lists to herself, commenting from time to time on how clear it all was, how easy to study this way.

"It's a museum of grammar," Shevi joked, and the girls laughed companionably.

A short while later, Shulamit knocked at the door. "Is Shevi home?"

"Come in, come in," I said with amusement.

"Hello, Shevi. Efrat! What are you doing here?"

Efrat smiled. "I came to study a bit with Shevi — isn't this the greatest system? It's so easy to study like this."

"To tell you the truth," Shulamit admitted, "I also came to check up on some rules of grammar I'm not sure of."

As she spoke, someone else knocked at the door. It seemed that Shevi's grammar charts were in demand. I smilingly admitted Rina, Michal, and Gili.

"Go right on in," I told them. "Shevi's holding court!"

I heard the girls all laughing and talking together. The word had swiftly spread that Shevi's home was decorated with the rules of grammar.

That's how the next few days passed. Shevi was awake early and stayed up late at night. She studied and reviewed and reviewed and studied, with and without the assistance of her friends.

Any other guest who happened to stop by for a visit was first astonished, then impressed with Shevi's "grammar museum." Abba explained proudly to one and all that his daughter was a dialysis patient who had missed out on most of her classes during the term, but was determined to take the examination with the rest of her class and, what's more, get a passing grade!

"We can all learn an important lesson from my daughter," he would tell the visitors. "You see what can be achieved if you only have the will to do it!"

Another refrain was heard at frequent intervals during those busy days and nights: "Shevi, eat something! Shevi, rest a little...." Mommy was anxious for Shevi not to overtax herself.

"Don't worry, Mommy," Shevi told her. "The studying itself gives me strength."

Exam day minus one. Shevi announced she would spend the entire day studying and do nothing else. To make up for not helping around the house, she promised cheerfully to do double, triple, or quadruple the amount of chores the next day. Did we need her help? The happiness that radiated from her was help enough for all of us.

"Yehudis, would you make up an exam for me to see if I know the material now?" With pleasure I spent half an hour or so writing out a full page of questions on Hebrew grammar for her to answer. Afterward we spent some time going over the points that still weren't clear, but she seemed to have mastered most of it.

"Shevi," I exclaimed in admiration, "you have caught up on several years' worth of study!" I found it hard to believe that two weeks earlier she hadn't understood a bit of it.

Exam day. We lined up to wish Shevi good luck as she left for school with Bashi. Mommy held out a package of chocolates with a note taped to it:

To my dear daughter Shevi,
With this I send my blessing to you:
May you succeed in all you do.
But fail or succeed, may you always cope,
and never despair, and never lose hope!
With love, Mommy.

That was just like Mommy — taking time to write something special, not just an ordinary note!

All the girls hurried to take their seats. The teacher passed out the test sheets and a heavy silence descended over the classroom. The girls bent over their desks, each wrapped in a cocoon of concentration. The teacher sat down at the front of the room and wished them a final, "Good luck!"

Shevi's hands were shaking; the words jumped on the page.

"Take it easy," she commanded herself. "Just relax and take a deep breath." She whispered a chapter of *Tehillim* to herself until she was calm enough to pick up her pen and begin to read the questions. Slowly, with gathering confidence, she began to fill in the answers.

An hour passed. Shevi was totally absorbed in the exam. She didn't see two of her sisters pause outside the door of the room and look in to see how she was doing. She never noticed the occasional glance of her good friend Michal, also checking up on her anxiously. Eventually most of the girls finished, and one by one handed in their tests.

Another fifteen minutes passed. Shevi raised her head at last and realized she was almost the only student left in the room. She panicked. What should she do? She was only about half-way through the test.

"You look upset, Shevi," Mrs. Greenberg said with real concern. "What's the matter?"

"I haven't finished yet," Shevi said, tears gathering in her eyes.

"Don't worry, Shevi, you have plenty of time." Mrs. Greenberg smiled understandingly. "At least another hour!"

Shevi was surprised, but she was so relieved she didn't question the teacher. She hastily picked up where she had left off, feeling renewed confidence: She still had a chance to do well. The answers flowed from her pen as she called up the images of her posters and lists. She filled in line after line, and didn't notice when the last of her classmates left the room.

At last she finished. She put down her pen and stood up slowly. She had done it!

"I...I'm sorry! I didn't expect the teacher to wait just for me...."

Mrs. Greenberg smiled. "That's my job," she said.

There aren't many teachers who would belittle the personal sacrifice involved in going out of their way to help a student with such good will and understanding.

CHAPTER TWENTY-SIX

ANOTHER OPERATION

❧ ❧

Shevi was napping in the afternoons again; her recent spurt of energy and initiative seemed to be ebbing rapidly. My parents were deeply concerned, for they suspected that the new kidney was no longer working.

"I think it's being rejected," Mommy said. "I've made an appointment with the specialist. We'll have to see what he says."

Naturally they were worried. If the kidney wasn't working, that meant it wasn't filtering the toxins out of Shevi's bloodstream, and she couldn't continue to walk around with all that poison in her system. Dynamic, ambitious, enthusiastic Shevi would once more be a helpless invalid. The tragedy of it struck deep in our hearts.

"I'm afraid she will have to start dialysis again," Mommy murmured.

Mommy and Shevi were walking home from the bus stop. It was a foggy morning with poor visibility — the buildings and greenery they passsed appeared blurred and indistinct. *That's an appropriate background to my state of mind at the moment,* Mommy reflected. *We can't foresee what the future will bring, we can't even predict what tomorrow will bring! I'm not so sure what the doctor will say this time, either.*

Shevi's thoughts, on the other hand, followed the flight of a bee buzzing past her head. *She's probably in a great hurry to collect*

*her nectar and rush back to the hive to make some honey. Everything
in the world has its purpose; the farmer hoes, the tailor sews.* Sometimes Shevi even thought in rhyme. *And I have to be strong and
take what comes and do the best I can,* she thought. She was determined not to let despair overwhelm her.

Mommy and Abba sat patiently outside the operating
room, praying that all would be well. Shevi's operation this time
was more difficult than previous ones. A special tube had to be
inserted in her abdomen to which the dialysis bags could be attached. This was a different technique — abdominal dialysis,
which presented new problems and untold torment for Shevi.
Mommy clutched her siddur in her hand and prayed to the Master of the Universe, "Let this chapter of Shevi's suffering be over
quickly; let them find a new kidney for her soon."

A nurse dressed in surgical green came through the doors
and said, "Mr. and Mrs. Wittow, the operation is over. You can
go into the recovery room for just a few minutes."

It was a large room with three or four patients lying on
gurneys, each of them hooked up to electronic monitors and an
intravenous apparatus. The beep of the monitors was continu-
ous, coming from all directions. Some of the patients were
groaning in pain. Shevi was lying on one of the gurneys. They
went over to her.

"Shevi? How do you feel?" Shevi looked at them in confusion, and a grimace of pain flickered across her face.

"The operation is over," Mommy said.

"Yes? It's over? That's good," she answered weakly.

"Everybody prayed for you," Abba told her.

"That's good. Thank you...." Her eyes closed.

"You'll have to leave now," a nurse told them kindly. "But
we'll let you know when she is transferred to her bed in the
ward."

In a few days, Shevi was able to come home. Abba had ordered dialysis bags for her, and when the delivery came, we were astonished to see tens and tens of boxes stacked high in the hallway.

"I hope Shevi won't need all of these," Bashi said quietly. "Let's pray that she can have another transplant soon."

Her prayers were answered sooner than we'd expected. Abba received the phone call notifying us that a kidney awaited her in Boston, Massachusetts, and he was instructed to make arrangements for the trip even before they were sure the kidney was compatible.

The kidney was compatible, and, as we described at the beginning of the book, Mommy and Shevi left in a headlong rush to get to Boston in time.

CHAPTER TWENTY-SEVEN

THE RACE TO BOSTON

&a &a

A ll the other passengers had already boarded when
Mommy and Shevi entered the plane, and the doors
swung shut immediately. With sighs of relief, Mommy and
Shevi sank into their seats. The first leg of their journey would
take them to Amsterdam. The plane taxied to its assigned run-
way and in a few more moments was in the air.

Shevi felt slightly dizzy and closed her eyes. She wasn't sure
if it was because of the rush, the change in air pressure at take-
off, or her emotional state before this third transplant operation. Mommy, too, was in a bit of a daze. She hardly heard the
stewardess come by and ask them what they would like to drink.

"Oh, er...two colas, please."

When the drinks were served and placed on the tray in
front of them, Mommy stared at them blankly for a few moments, then started to cry quietly.

"Mommy! Why are you crying?" Shevi asked. She wanted
to say, "We should be happy..." but she started to cry, too.

After a while they blotted their tears with tissues and were
able to sip their drinks. Shevi had never seen her mother in such
a state and wasn't sure how to handle it. Finally, she offered her
some chocolate from the package they'd bought at the airport,
but that set them off again. They comforted each other with
hugs and sat quietly in their seats, unable to speak during most
of the flight.

The plane for London was waiting for them in Amsterdam.

An airline agent boarded as soon as they rolled to a stop to help them hurry off one plane and onto another. The hospital in Boston had been in touch with the airlines and stressed the urgency of the situation, so the London plane had been waiting for half an hour.

As soon as they were seated in the second plane, it took off. The steward wished them a good trip...and good luck with the transplant operation. He went forward onto the flight deck and they sank back in their seats. Shevi saw that Mommy was weeping again, and that set her off. They more or less cried together quietly all the way to London.

In London they disembarked and hurried off to catch the plane to New York.

The American Airlines stewardess welcomed them aboard with a warm smile.

"We've been waiting for you; the hospital in Boston told us you were on your way. The main thing is, you're here now and we can take off. Come with me." She showed them to their seats.

This would be a longer flight than the two short European "hops" and they managed to settle down and take out things to read. Mommy had bought an English book at the airport, and Shevi had a children's book in her purse — the large letters were suitable for times when it was difficult to concentrate.

The stewardess was attentive; they were served drinks and a kosher meal. They tried to distract themselves by reading, but their thoughts were fastened on the impending operation. Would they arrive in time? Would the transplant succeed? Would Shevi at last begin to grow a bit taller? Maybe it was too late for that, but maybe....

"Fasten your seat belts, please. We are about to land at John F. Kennedy Airport, in New York. You must remain in your seats until the plane has stopped moving."

Now there was just one more plane to catch. Mommy and

Shevi prepared themselves for the next dash — to Boston; there only a taxi ride to the hospital awaited them.

They rushed, flight bags in hand, out of the plane, through the enclosed gangway to the waiting room, down the steps and out to the airfield, up the steps of still one more plane.

"We're happy to see you," the stewardess smiled. "The rest of the passengers don't know why we are delayed, but I'm sure you know the hospital in Boston has instructed us to wait for you. Come, sit down and catch your breath...and good luck!"

"Another hour, and this nightmare of a trip will be over," Shevi sighed.

Mommy started to agree with Shevi, but once more the tears started to flow. Mommy had always been the strong, brave one who kept everyone's spirits up, but on this trip it seemed that fear had overwhelmed her. Also, it must be remembered, Mommy did not at all enjoy traveling.

"Mommy," Shevi suddenly turned to Mommy, "do you forgive me?"

"What do you mean? What should I forgive you for, Shevi?"

"I hope you aren't angry with me...."

"Angry? Forgive? What is this all about?"

"I feel terrible that...you have to go through so much...because of me. All the running back and forth to doctors and hospitals, and all the worrying." She stopped to blow her nose. "And now, now you are even missing Tovah Leah's engagement party because of me." She started to sob. "You're not going to be at Tovah Leah's engagement party because of me."

Mommy was stunned. She hugged Shevi. "Shevi, you're wrong! Did you decide that the date of the transplant should be the same day as Tovah Leah's engagement? Of course not! It's not you who's causing us all this running around! There is a Creator who is running the world. He decides when I have to run around, when I should worry and how much. *Baruch Hashem,*

He decided the transplant would be on her engagement day and not on her wedding day!"

Mommy put her arm around Shevi's shaking shoulders. "Hashem is the One Who decides everything that goes on in the world. He decides who...will live and who...will die; who will become ill and who will get well...." Mommy's voice broke. "And Hashem is the One Who gave me you! I'm happy with the treasure Hashem has given me. I wouldn't trade a precious daughter like you for anyone else in the world...even a healthy daughter! You are my own wonderful daughter and you aren't causing me any trouble or problems. I thank Hashem that He gave you to me. Even if I am a bit worried and upset, thank God it is for a precious girl like you!"

Their tears mingled as they hugged each other tightly. Those were moments of deep importance, of incomparable devotion and steadfast faith...faith in the One who manages the world, who changes times and who alters seasons...and who heals those who are ill.

"Ladies and gentlemen, fasten your seat belts, please. We are approaching Logan Airport in Boston, Massachusetts, and will be on the ground in a few minutes. The time in Boston is 11:55 P.M. and the weather is...."

The passengers fastened their seat belts, glanced at their watches, repacked their briefcases and flight bags. A little boy clapped his hands and chanted to himself, "We're here! We're here!" A little blond-haired, blue-eyed girl grinned at Shevi and confided, "I'm going to see my Grandma." Shevi smiled back with warmth.

Mommy and Shevi swallowed hard and sat up straight in their seats. The trip was almost over, but now the difficult part would begin: a new chapter in pain and suffering, blood transfusions, injections, painkillers, bleeping machines....

As they walked off the exit ramp, a smiling woman approached them and said, "You must be Shevi and Hannah Wittow, right? My name is Sheila and I'm going to take you to the hospital. My car is parked outside. Come, let's hurry — they're waiting for you at the hospital, and I have the honor of being your guide."

Honor? thought Shevi with astonishment. *She makes it seem as if we are doing her a favor by agreeing to let her take us where we want to go.* Shevi was reminded of a saying of the Sages: More than the master of the house does for the beggar, the beggar does for the master of the house. This woman certainly personified that maxim. A total stranger was prepared to chauffeur them to the hospital — and on top of that, she made it seem as if it was a pleasure for her to go to all that trouble to help them.

"Do you know," Mommy told Sheila, "someone at the hospital called the airlines, and each of our connections was waiting for us all along the way."

"I know," Sheila said. "That was Dr. Shapiro's transplant coordinator, Joan Abrams. She is amazing. She makes all the arrangements for the transplant patients. You'll meet her tomorrow."

They sped past tree-lined sidewalks, past neat, red-brick homes surrounded by trim lawns bordered with flowering bushes and two large cars parked in almost every driveway. Shevi was entranced, forgetting for the moment where she was going and what awaited her there. They pulled up to the emergency entrance of a huge hospital complex.

"Here we are," Sheila announced. "Beth Israel Hospital."

"Thank you so very much, Sheila," Mommy said appreciatively. Sheila dismissed the thanks with a wave of her hand and wished them good luck.

"Hurry," said a nurse who was apparently waiting especially for them. "Lie down on the gurney, Miss Wittow; the attendant is taking you directly to the operating room."

"But I can walk," Shevi objected.

A muscular young man — his name tag said "Steve"— relieved Shevi of her flight bag, stored it underneath, and helped Shevi to lie down on the wheeled stretcher. They moved rapidly toward an elevator, and Mommy and the nurse rushed after them.

They emerged from the elevator directly in front of a large, swinging, double door marked "Surgery — Authorized Personnel Only."

"Hello!" A tall, lean doctor with smiling blue eyes approached them. "So here you are at last. I'm Dr. Michael Shapiro, your surgeon."

Shevi was relieved to meet such a friendly doctor. It certainly was reassuring.

Another doctor came over to Shevi with a blood-pressure cuff. "Hold out your arm, please. My name is Dr. Grant." He was smiling, too.

Smiles, Shevi thought, *are so soothing. If only I could package some smiles from important doctors and import them to Israel to give to some doctors I know there!* The idea amused her.

"You look pretty happy," Dr. Shapiro said with surprise.

"She is happy," Mommy said with a wink to Shevi. "Shevi likes American things, and now she'll have an American kidney!"

The doctors and nurses surrounding Shevi, quite a crowd by now, all laughed, even as they attached her to the intravenous apparatus.

"Boy, that was quick," Shevi said. "I hardly felt a thing."

"You'll be feeling plenty, don't worry," Dr. Grant encouraged her.

Steve pushed open the door to the surgery room and wheeled Shevi in. "This is as far as you can come, ma'am," he said politely to Mommy, looking at her with compassion in his eyes. "Usually they prep the transplant patients in the ward beforehand, but they told me this is an emergency and not to waste any time." He gave a little cough. "Um...I hope the operation is a success, ma'am, and that the kidney will be accepted." He walked out.

Before long, Shevi was attached to a blood-pressure monitor and an electrocardiograph machine.

"That's it for now," said a pink-cheeked young nurse. "We've decked you out enough."

Shevi's expression was serious now. She lay quietly, her heart pounding. She was praying that the operation would be successful and that the kidney would be accepted.

Mommy sat in the ward, saying *Tehillim* and waiting for Shevi to awaken from the anesthesia. Shevi was heavily bandaged and lay still, a small figure in an immense bed. Waves of pain pounded at her, and she was only minimally aware of her surroundings. Mommy sat there patiently, listening to the birds singing on the windowsill for quite some time.

"Mommy..." Shevi croaked in a weak voice.

At last! Mommy jumped up and leaned over the bed.

"Oh, Shevi, I was getting worried."

"Mommy, what's wrong with me? Why can't I move? Why does everything hurt?"

"*Mazal tov*, Shevi! The operation is over. You have a new kidney."

"O...over? New...kidney? I won't need...abdominal dialysis anymore? I'll be able to eat regular food? I can't believe it...."

"How do you feel?"

Shevi smiled through the pain. "I feel fine! I'm very happy...and that gives me strength to overcome...the pain...."

Even as Mommy stood there, Shevi suddenly turned pale, her lips trembled, and her eyes closed. She became whiter, and it looked as if she had fainted.

"Shevi! Shevi, can you hear me?" Mommy reached for Shevi's hand: it was icy cold. "Nurse! Nurse!" she yelled, jabbing the alarm button frantically. "Help!"

Immediately doctors and nurses rushed in and within a few seconds, Shevi was surrounded by emergency equipment. Mommy was shouldered aside and they worked over Shevi, trying to revive her. Mommy felt as if her heart had stopped beating. She prayed silently, "Please, Hashem, don't take my little girl!"

Slowly, gradually, color returned to Shevi's face; her eyelids fluttered. The doctors breathed sighs of relief.

"What happened?" Mommy asked. She was white and shaking.

"We almost lost her," a frightened nurse answered.

Dr. Shapiro took off his glasses, removed a handkerchief from his pocket, and slowly mopped his forehead. Then he polished his steamed-over glasses.

"The pain weakened her," he explained. "She was simply too weak to cope with all that pain." He took a deep breath. "But it's all right now. She is over the worst." He spent several minutes reassuring Mommy before he left the room.

Mommy was limp with relief, but she was extremely impressed with what she had just seen. "What doctors! How wonderfully they treat their patients. It's so satisfying to see doctors who treat their patients like people, not numbers. Hashem's kindness is never-ending. Here I am alone in a strange place; I don't know a soul. And Hashem in His goodness has sent us such wonderful doctors and nurses to help at such a difficult time."

Little did Mommy dream that this was just the surface of the ocean of kindness and remarkably selfless assistance she and Shevi were to receive during the time they spent in Boston. No, she wasn't alone at all. Hashem, in His mercy, had planted so many good-hearted people there. She would come to know the Boston Jewish community well, especially the organization of volunteers that worked with the Bostoner Rebbe, *shlita*, and extended a helping hand to so many people who arrived in Boston with life-threatening illnesses.

CHAPTER TWENTY-EIGHT

NOT FOR MY SAKE!

ళ ళ

Shevi examined the printed forms in her hand. It was a few days after the operation and, thank God, though she still suffered great pain, she was now able to sit up in bed and eat normal meals. Mommy was, as usual, sitting next to the bed. Edna, a perky Jamaican nurse, had just passed out forms to all the patients. "Just fill these in; you can choose whatever you like for each meal, and we'll come by to collect the cards in a little while," she said, and continued on her rounds.

Shevi was a bit confused. What was this all about? Pick whatever she liked? They were apparently two menu cards with boxes to check off next to each item. There was a long list of choices for the main course: chicken cacciatore, beef goulash, broiled steak, sweet and sour meatballs, and hamburger patties. An assortment of salads followed that: chopped liver, potato salad, noodle salad, Waldorf salad, vegetable salad. For dessert there was a choice of Boston cream cake, blintzes, chocolate mousse, raspberry sherbert, and applesauce.

Shevi looked at Mommy in perplexity. "This must be very expensive, don't you think? This can hardly be regular hospital food."

Mommy stood up and took the two cards over to the nurses' station. "What are we supposed to do with these cards?" she asked.

"Those are menus. Don't you read English? You sound like an American." The nurse was a rosy-cheeked young woman whose name tag read, appropriately: Rosie.

"Well, yes, I was born in the United States. But this looks like a fancy hotel menu, not a hospital menu."

Rosie laughed and said cheerfully, "That's right! Welcome to our hotel! No, I'm joking. Don't you know the procedure for meals here? Don't they have this system in Israel?"

"Hardly!" Mommy answered. "Do you mind coming back to the room with me and explaining this to my daughter as well?" The two returned to the room to include Shevi in the conversation.

"All that food mentioned on the cards is making me hungry," Shevi informed them with a twinkle in her eye.

"That's wonderful," Rosie smiled. "That's a good sign."

"A good appetite is how you tell — if a person is feeling well!" Shevi rhymed.

"Shevi, you are something else!" laughed Rosie. "Look here, this card is for you to order whatever food you may want to eat during the day, for breakfast, lunch, and supper. You just mark off the box next to your choice. This card is for you and this one is for your mother."

"For me, too? I don't believe this!" Mommy was astonished.

"Don't you have to eat, too?" asked Rosie with good humor. "All we need is for you to faint from hunger right here in the hospital! Really, we know how a devoted mother like you stays right by her child and sometimes doesn't eat a thing all day. We can't have that."

"I'm so glad you told us," Shevi said. "Now I can really enjoy my meals. Whenever I'm in the hospital my mother watches me eat and tries to get me to eat everything, and I just can't do it knowing she hasn't had anything but Coca-Cola all day."

Rosie patted Mommy on the hand and went out. Mommy and Shevi happily turned their attention to the task of choosing their meals. Not only was the choice like that of a five-star hotel, but the type of *hechsher* was marked next to each dish! This was the height of luxury and comfort, for which they could no doubt thank the efforts of the Jewish community in Boston. Knowing that her mother would not have to go out looking for a place to eat lifted Shevi's spirits and made it a bit easier for her to bear the pain.

At twelve o'clock a young man knocked on the door and came in carrying two pink plastic trays, each sealed in cellophane-wrap. "Are you Batsheva and Hannah Wittow?" he asked. When they nodded their heads, he put the trays down on the bedside table and took a pad and pencil from his pocket. "Just sign here," he indicated a place on the page.

Mommy signed for both of them, and he pocketed the pad and pencil. "Get well soon!" he said cheerfully as he left.

"What wonderful service!" Shevi said in appreciation. "People just don't realize what a positive effect good treatment and a pleasant attitude can have on a sick person. I truly believe that this kind of attitude makes the healing go faster."

She thought for a few moments and then added, "We have to learn from this, I think, that we should always treat others kindly, even when we're not in a good mood or feeling well ourselves! We just don't realize how much we can give to others when we.... But I'm talking and talking and you're not eating, Mommy."

"You are right, though. Those are very important thoughts," Mommy said approvingly.

"As if they were something new to you," Shevi responded. "You always treat people with warmth and a smile. I've never seen you in a 'bad' mood, even when you are tired." Shevi took Mommy's hand and squeezed it fondly.

"I'll be getting fat from compliments," Mommy laughed. "Compliments are full of calories, so I won't be able to eat all the delicious food we ordered." Laughing together companionably, they uncovered their trays and began to eat.

"Everything is so delicious," Shevi said.

It's been so long, Mommy thought, *since I've seen her enjoy a meal. I hope that's a sign that she is really beginning to get well.*

"Chicken, liver, and meat — taste better than a sweet," Shevi rhymed. "It's been so long since I've tasted chicken or meat."

The image of Shevi lying on the sofa in our living room appeared to Mommy: Shevi pleading to be excused from eating, saying over and over that she had no appetite. Not even a special dish that she used to love to eat could tempt her...she just had no appetite. Those had been difficult times for Mommy, times when Shevi's condition was deteriorating rapidly and nothing seemed to help. Now she basked in the sight of Shevi's enjoyment of her food, at the healthy color returning to Shevi's face.

They spent the rest of the afternoon contentedly playing Twenty Questions.

For two weeks Mommy slept at night on a folding cot in Shevi's room and sat on a chair all day. They had few visitors: Uncle Herman's daughter Amy; Mommy's sister Sheba; Abba's niece Shana, and the faithful volunteer Sheila, who came by regularly to see how they were getting along.

One morning Sheila told Mommy she thought it was time for her to start sleeping in a regular bed again.

"It's not too bad here," Mommy said. "I'm comfortable enough."

"If you'd said that on the telephone, I might have believed you," Sheila answered. "But I can see in person how tired you are, what dark circles you have under your eyes. In fact, that's one of the reasons I stopped by this morning. Of course, the main reason was to visit Shevi," she said with a wink at Shevi.

Such a nice lady! Shevi thought.

"But...but...." Mommy didn't know what to say.

"I'll bet you're worried about where to stay and how to get

back and forth from the hospital, right?"

Mommy nodded.

"Don't give it a second thought!" Sheila said. "You've heard about the Bostoner Rebbe's *chesed* organization Rofeh, I'm sure. Well, Leon Katsoff, who is in charge of the office, has organized a place for you in our guest house. He's the one who sent me to the airport to pick you up and he's the one who organized your Shabbos meals in the hospital, and he's fixed up the apartment for you. I have a list of ladies who are ready and willing to pick you up and deliver you, to drive you to and from the hospital whenever you like. All you have to do is pick up the phone and call one of our volunteers and she will arrange transportation. One of our volunteer drivers is practically always on call."

Mommy and Shevi were overwhelmed. Such kindness! Such wonderful people! All of them just waiting to do good deeds and help others. It was a great comfort to know they were surrounded by friends in a strange city.

"Well? How about it?" Sheila urged.

Mommy looked at Shevi. Should she leave her alone in the hospital? It was a difficult decision.

"Go ahead, Mommy," Shevi said. "It will be so good for you to get a good night's sleep." As she spoke it was apparent that a sudden wave of pain engulfed her, though she tried to smile bravely and conceal it from her mother. Her heart started to pump faster, but she didn't say a word.

"Oh, Shevi, you are in pain, aren't you? Don't pretend that it doesn't hurt."

"Listen, Mommy, an operation is an operation — I have to feel something."

Sheila felt the tension in the room and decided to leave. She said she would return later, if all was well, to take Mommy to the Rofeh guest house.

Mommy sat down again, resting her swollen feet on the low stepstool next to the bed. She looked intently at Shevi.

Shevi looked well enough, but Mommy sensed that something was wrong, that something was not quite as it should be, though she could not pinpoint what it was.

"Go ahead, Mommy, really. After all, I'm not a baby."

Mommy rested her hand on Shevi's. "Shevi! You must tell me what the matter is!" Mommy sounded angry and her hands were trembling.

Shevi was confused. She wanted so much to do the right thing, to encourage Mommy to get some much-needed rest, but now Mommy was angry with her. Mommy was already pressing the buzzer to call the nurse.

Rosie appeared in the doorway. "What's the problem?"

"Shevi doesn't feel well," Mommy said with a worried frown on her forehead.

Rosie immediately felt for Shevi's pulse and timed it. Then she took the cuff from its hook on the wall and tested her blood pressure. "I'll be right back," she said and hurried out of the room.

Shevi was trying to understand what was happening to her. She didn't want to make Mommy angry, she wanted to apologize...but the room started to spin around...Mommy was spinning around, too...now she was near, now far away. She tried to tell Mommy she was sorry, but no sound emerged.

A team of doctors and nurses came in and competently set to work on Shevi. "Her blood pressure is up and her pulse is not steady," one of the doctors explained to Mommy.

Mommy turned pale. *Oh, no!* she screamed silently. *She was doing so well, she can't be getting worse! How much more does she have to suffer? Hasn't she suffered enough? Please,* she prayed, *I know all is for the best, but please let her stop suffering; please grant her good health, please let her walk together with her friends once again.*

The doctors were working busily over Shevi, but Mommy had her eyes closed, praying. Shevi lay quietly back and said her own prayers, even as the injection pierced her skin. "Hashem, give me strength to bear this! Let me be healthy, not for my own sake, but for my poor long-suffering mother's sake. Make me well for my devoted, loving mother!"

The two silent prayers originating in that hospital room rose higher and higher until they fused into one heartrending, fervent supplication.

CHAPTER TWENTY-NINE

COMPASSION

ৰ্থ ৰ্থ

The hours passed slowly. Mommy was in the same exhausted position on the chair in Shevi's room; her head rested on the back of the chair, her feet up on the footstool. Her face was pale and her eyes were closed, but she wasn't sleeping. She knew that Shevi was in critical condition; how could she sleep? She was aware that nurses were quietly coming and going, but she didn't see Sheila looking in at her from the doorway.

Sheila was accustomed to hospital procedure and had witnessed many a crisis in the course of her volunteer work for the Rebbe, *shlita*. She went directly to the head nurse to find out what the situation was. The head nurse told her gently that there had been a complication and they were not yet sure exactly what had happened. They knew the patient had taken a turn for the worse and they were doing everything possible to diagnose the problem quickly. "They might have to do a biopsy, and that is not a good sign."

Sheila thanked her and said she would return later.

More time passed. Shevi slept. The intravenous tube slowly infused antibiotics into her bloodstream to counteract whatever infection might have taken root. Her face was ashen, but her labored breathing was slowly returning to normal.

"Mrs. Wittow!" A voice gently penetrated Mommy's daze. Rosie was standing beside her with a doctor. "This is Dr. Terry Strom, chief nephrologist of Beth Israel. He wants to explain what's happened."

"Hello, Shevi, Mrs. Wittow." Shevi was awake now and he felt for Shevi's pulse while he spoke. "We have some test results in hand now, but we have decided we must do a further test, a very difficult one, I'm sorry to say, but necessary. We have to examine the status of Shevi's kidney...we have to make sure it isn't being rejected." He spoke softly and with great compassion.

"No, no! Don't say that!" Shevi cried out in alarm. "Don't tell me the kidney is being rejected again! Don't tell me you're going to do a...a...."

She began to sob. Dr. Strom was startled. He knew Shevi to be a calm patient, who never complained, never cried and certainly never shouted.

"...just not a biopsy!" she pleaded.

"How did you know that we need to do a biopsy, Shevi?" he asked in astonishment. "You'll soon be qualified to be on our staff."

Mommy tried to lighten the atmosphere, saying, "Who knows? Maybe Shevi will be a kidney specialist one day. She certainly knows enough on the subject already. She won't have to consult the medical books, she can just consult her memory!"

They all smiled except Shevi. "Yes, and the memory is most unpleasant! I will never forget the biopsy they did after the first transplant failed. It was pure agony! And then, to hear that the kidney was rejected! And to be told I'd have to wait for another kidney...."

Dr. Strom, Rosie, and Mommy were shocked into silence. They searched for the right words to say, but found none. Shevi herself was in shock. She looked around at everyone, until her tear-filled eyes rested on Mommy and registered Mommy's expression of sadness and pain. Her deeply compassionate soul would not allow her to witness her mother's pain. She suppressed her own hurt and found the words to comfort her mother.

Smiling bravely through her tears, she said, "Well, Mommy,

you always tell me that I seem to find a great deal of variety in my life; sometimes it's an operation on my hand, sometimes on my stomach, sometimes on my throat. I try not to let things get boring, right?" They could hardly believe their ears.

"So, this time...the results of the biopsy just have to be different! For the sake of variety! It's a good thing the results of the other biopsy were negative, so that this time they can be positive!"

The others all sighed in relief. Shevi had done it again. Through her own pain and distress she had found the words to change her mother's frown to a smile and lift the mood of everyone around her.

Mommy could not conceal her pride in Shevi. Dr. Strom shook his head in wonder. "You have a most unusual daughter," he said.

Rosie patted Shevi's hand, the one that was not attached to the intravenous tube. "You're going to be someone special when you grow up," she said in admiration.

"She already is!" exclaimed Edna, who had heard Shevi's cries and came in to help. "We can all take a lesson from Shevi! Now you just lie back and relax, honey, till the stretcher gets here." All the medical personnel left then, and Shevi tried to compose herself and stay calm. Mommy spoke to her quietly and they waited together, as they had waited so many times before, for Shevi to be taken to the operating room.

When the hospital attendant lifted her onto the gurney a little while later, Shevi cheerfully waved goodbye and was wheeled away with a broad smile on her face, as if she didn't know what an unpleasant experience awaited her. She was a tiny, brave figure, facing the inevitable like a tough soldier marching off to battle. Shevi knew very well what a painful procedure a kidney biopsy is; she had suffered through it before. She hadn't ever told Mommy how bad it was. A thick needle is inserted deep into the body until it reaches the kidney. It removes a microscopic piece of kidney tissue and no anesthesia is used to help the patient endure it. The pain is indescribable, excruciating, and unforgettable. That piece of tissue is then tested. And all the while, the patient is trembling with fright and praying that the test will be positive, that the kidney has been accepted.

Mommy was sitting on a chair outside the operating room. Again. The rain drummed on the window in tempo with the pounding of her heart. The gray and cloudy sky she glimpsed through the windows matched her mood. Time seemed to stand still; whenever she glanced at the wall clock it seemed the hands had not moved at all. Her lips moved in prayer. "Please, O Lord, send a quick and full recovery to all Your people who are ill."

Dr. Strom came out of the operating room, still dressed in his green sterile working clothes. He released the surgical mask from behind one ear and let it hang down so he could speak.

"Mrs. Wittow, you have nothing to worry about." He smiled and sighed deeply. "The kidney is okay. It has not been rejected and is functioning. We can increase Shevi's medication now to help prevent rejection and strengthen it. Things look good." He turned and reentered the operating room.

"*Baruch Hashem,*" Mommy sighed in relief. "Thank God it's all right."

Meanwhile, the doctors kept Shevi in the recovery room to track her reaction to the biopsy. She lay on the gurney, exhausted, her skin as white as the sheet she was covered with. A nurse stood by to moisten Shevi's lips and monitor her pulse and blood pressure. It had been such an enervating, harrowing, painful procedure that Shevi had momentarily forgotten her concern about the results.

When they told her the good news, she shivered in relief. Her eyes lit up and she even managed to smile. She felt a wave of happiness well up within her and fill her pain-racked body. "My kidney is working." What beautiful words. "Please, Hashem,

You who search man's kidneys and heart, please watch over my new kidney...take care of it...let it filter my blood as it should...and I...I promise I'll filter all my deeds and not let self-ishness or pride contaminate them.... I will not let *lashon hara* destroy my soul...." Her eyes began to close. "I'll strain out all the impurities within me...I'll sift carefully each and every thing I do...."

Shevi slept.

Roses were blooming in Shevi's cheeks. Her eyes were once again a deep, lustrous green, shining with happiness. Her health was returning, slowly, but visibly. She was still getting medication intravenously and she was still getting injections in her arm regularly, but she was able to start conducting visits to other patients to cheer them up. That was typically Shevi.

A young girl lay in another room. Shevi went to visit her, trailing her intravenous apparatus. "Hello, Miriam. How are you today?"

Miriam looked at Shevi with large, dark, sad eyes. "I feel so weak; I have no strength," she answered.

Shevi sat down. "Be strong, Miriam," she said. "Sometimes we think we've reached the end of our rope, that we simply can't take any more. Then, suddenly...."

Miriam was paying close attention.

"...God gives us strength and He helps us to cope with our problems."

Miriam had to smile at Shevi's optimism. "You talk as if it is all behind you."

"Not all," Shevi answered. "No, not all. But a lot is behind me now, *Baruch Hashem!*"

CHAPTER THIRTY

FRIENDSHIP

☙ ☙

Shevi stayed in the hospital for about four weeks, but the doctors wanted her to remain in Boston for at least another two and a half weeks.

Abba had flown over about a week and a half previously, but he had contracted a terrible cold and was not allowed to go near Shevi. With his usual enterprise, he arranged to spend some time recuperating — in Denver, Colorado, while visiting Grandma Wittow!

Now he returned to Boston and was able to help Shevi and Mommy get settled in their apartment in the Rofeh guest house, and spend a few happy days with them before returning to Israel. Shevi felt great! She walked out of the hospital an entirely different person from the one who had entered. She was the picture of good health and she was ready to indulge her and Mommy's love of shopping and have a good time. One day cousin Amy came to take them shopping in Filene's famous Basement and then out to lunch in a restaurant. Another day one of the volunteers was driving to New York City and offered them a ride, which they accepted with alacrity. Mommy's close friend from high school, Gloria Katz, took them around Boro Park and in not much more than four hours (that was all the time they had!) they managed to purchase an entire trousseau for Tovah Leah. Not only did Shevi keep up with them, but she appeared to have even more stamina than Mommy.

Two and a half weeks after being released from the hospital, Shevi was on her way home. We couldn't wait to see our sister again. Mommy had called home regularly to keep us apprised of Shevi's health and progress after the transplant operation. We'd suffered with her during the terrible, critical moments, and rejoiced with her when Shevi started to recuperate.

Shevi was coming home! We were all there at the airport waiting to greet them. We knew that Shevi's ever-optimistic nature would not permit her to dwell on the pain she'd suffered, but rather she'd tell us how well she felt, how thankful she was about everything. She had gone away so pale and sick, and she'd return refreshed and renewed. All pain would be forgotten, the bad times leaving not a trace. Her tiny hand would wipe clean the enormous slate of suffering.

The house was cleaned and polished to the best of our ability — it wouldn't do to have Mommy come home to a messy apartment. There were fresh flowers in vases on every table; our friends had sent them in honor of Shevi's return. Shevi's friends had baked cakes and they were all on display on the dining room table. The phone was ringing constantly with people asking excitedly if Shevi had arrived yet.

When Shevi left the house for the first time after her return, her heart was filled with gratitude as she drank in all the familiar sights: the street, the trees, the buses, the passersby, the Jerusalem skyline. Bashi had urged her to go to the grocery store to buy some milk, but every few steps she had to stop and greet one friend after another who came over to hug and kiss her and say how much she had been missed. Shevi's heart swelled with joy.

Her friend Penina caught Shevi's hand in hers. "Come up to my house with me, please, Shevi," she begged.

"But your family..." Shevi hesitated.

"My family? My family will be thrilled to see you. My mother is so happy you're back, and Saraleh will jump for joy. They all missed you so much — why don't you want to come up?"

"All right," Shevi decided. She had to gather her courage around her like a shield, but she was determined to overcome her shyness and accept being the center of attention for once. They rode to the top floor in the elevator; one girl bubbling over with excitement, the other fighting off her fear of being on show. She hoped Penina's younger brothers and sisters hadn't forgotten her and wouldn't laugh when they saw her again.

The door flew open and Mrs. Lev and Saraleh were holding out their arms to welcome her. They embraced her warmly and affectionately, and ushered her into their small apartment. Shevi saw the glint of a tear in Mrs. Lev's eye, and that tear seemed to her like a well of clear, refreshing water in the desert. That single tear of emotion watered her tired heart, turned the arid reaches of her past fears and disappointments into a meadow of hope and encouragement and strengthened her resolve to go ever forward and to persevere, despite the obstacles.

They sat Shevi down in the dining room and brought out a platter of cake and tall glasses of iced tea. "Sit down," Shevi pleaded. "Don't wait on me like this."

"You haven't seen anything yet!" said Penina's older sister Riva, entering with a three-tiered cake, iced in blue and white with a map of Eretz Yisrael outlined on top in chocolate. "See what Penina baked in honor of your return home. It's just been sitting here waiting for you to set foot in our house."

"It is absolutely gorgeous," Shevi said. "But...how did you know when...."

"I asked your sisters to make sure you'd go downstairs just so I could accidentally meet you in the street. I've been planning this for days," Penina said.

So that was the purpose of the sudden need for milk at home! It wasn't like her sisters to make her go...she had wondered why they hadn't gone themselves.

"It's...good to be here," she said shyly. "I wasn't expecting such a reception."

"Shevi, you can't imagine how we've been thinking of you all the time, knowing you were in Boston, in a strange place, and having such a hard time," Penina said emotionally.

"We prayed to Hashem," added Mrs. Lev warmly, "that you'd be freed from your never-ending dialysis once and for all." And she kissed Shevi's cheek.

Shevi was simply overwhelmed with good feeling as she gazed around her at this warm, loving family — her friends. What wonderful people, what good-hearted friends Hashem has blessed her with. More valuable than silver or gold, she thought: friendship!

The rain poured down in torrents; the wind lashed at the bare trees and howled through the slits in the shutters. In the Wittow apartment silence reigned; everyone slept — well, almost everyone. Mommy turned in her sleep; a faint sound disturbed her and she sat up to listen. It was 2:00 A.M. She rose and put on her robe and slippers and quietly left the bedroom.

"Shevi? What's the matter?" The light was on in the kitchen and Shevi was sitting there crying.

"N...nothing's the matter, Mommy. I'm fine," she sniffed.

"Why are you crying, then? Did someone say something hurtful to you today?"

"No, nothing like that, Mommy. Actually, my friends have been wonderful. I never dreamed I'd have such a tremendous welcome."

"Tell me, then. Please tell me," Mommy urged her.

"Mommy," Shevi sighed. "I was thinking about little Tali, who is still in the dialysis ward. I can't...it's so hard to think that I am healthy now and Tali...still has to have dialysis all the time."

A few simple words, but what an enormous measure of sensitivity they revealed. A towering soul housed in such a tiny body.

CHAPTER THIRTY-ONE

THE MORE THINGS CHANGE...

ॐ ॐ

*F*rom the height of well-being and contentment, Shevi was tossed once again to the depths of anguish and embarrassment. We had momentarily basked in the light of Shevi's warm welcome by her close friends and family and felt deeply moved by her pleasure. However, ordinary life went on, and though Shevi was delighted to be back in harness at school, that did not mean that all the wretched torments of her existence had magically disappeared.

We were attending the wedding of a dear friend; we girls were extremely attached to the bride and our family to her family as well. The wedding hall was elegantly decorated, the tables laden with tasty salads, and the linens and cutlery were colorfully matched and sparkling. The groom came to cover his bride's face with the veil before the *chuppah* and the guests quieted down. The procession to the *chuppah* put everyone in a state of high emotion, and we all stood crowded together in the courtyard of the hotel, trying to follow the proceedings under the *chuppah*.

"That lady's so fat I can't see!" A rude, childish voice shocked us.

"Oooh, see the midget. Isn't she funny-looking?" Another voice shocked us even more. I whirled around and saw a gaggle of little girls surrounding Shevi and laughing at her. Shevi was transfixed; her enormous green eyes looked at me with mortifi-

cation and helplessness. The girls laughed again. Shevi turned
red with embarrassment and I — I was just furious!

"Are you Jewish?" I asked the girls indignantly. "You're be-
having like little Nazis," I managed to choke out before putting
my arm around Shevi and pulling her into the hall. Mommy
and our sisters rallied around and accompanied Shevi inside
and over to the table we had reserved. Shevi was crying, her face
blanched and her hands shaking.

"I'm going home," she said in a voice so low we could
hardly hear her. "I can't stay here."

"Shevi, please stay."

"No, I don't think I can. It's not...good for me to stay. I was
looking forward so much to being at this wedding...." Tears
choked her. "But what can I do when there are people who treat
me like...that?"

I'd hardly ever seen her cry in public like this.

"Shevi," Mommy said. "If you go, I'm going too."

Esther quickly said, "Shevi, please stay for Mommy's sake."

We sat there silently for a few moments, looking at each
other indecisively. Then Shevi visibly pulled herself together
and with a great effort smiled through her tears at Mommy.
"Okay. I'll stay. So let's go and wash for the meal, what are we
waiting for?"

What a mitzvah! Shevi was the living personification of the
commandment to honor your parents. She would do anything
for Mommy's sake. We saw how she wanted to go home and recover from the searing humiliation she had just suffered, but
she would stay so that Mommy's enjoyment of the *simchah* was
not ruined, and she would even try to enjoy herself, not just
pretend to enjoy herself, to cheer Mommy. Is it any wonder that
Mommy regarded Shevi as a most precious gift from God?

The dancing began. We joined in, but Shevi stayed at the table. We were able to forget the incident and join heartily in the
dancing. We even forgot that Shevi was sitting there alone, that

she had to be guarded against a repetition of the cruel, heartless teasing. We were having a good time.

Penina saw us and came over to ask where Shevi was. Shevi? Why, Shevi was still sitting all alone at our table. We looked over and saw that she was definitely not at ease. I felt so guilty; how could we have left her like that? It must be so uncomfortable to sit by yourself at a wedding with everyone around dancing or chatting with friends. To be so alone....

"Shevi, why don't you come and dance?" I asked her.

"No, I don't think so. Look, I'm not afraid of those little girls. Really! I...oh, dancing just isn't for me."

"Oh, it's not for you, huh? Well, it's not for me, either; it's for the bride," I said sharply. I don't know why, but sometimes I wanted to make her angry, to goad her into expressing her anger, to make her talk it out.

"Yehudis, now that's enough!" she cried angrily.

"Shevi, I'm sorry. Really, why aren't you dancing?"

"Well, you know, when everyone is dancing so fast, with such abandon, I...I always just get stepped on and sort of trampled. People don't notice that I'm dancing too, that I'm also a person...."

"Oh, come on," I said. "You're not that tiny."

"I know. But that's what always happens," she said as she stood up.

"I'll dance right next to you," I assured her.

"You'll see," she said resignedly.

I can hardly bring myself to recount what happened. We joined a circle and began to dance to the joyous music. More women and girls came into the circle, expanding it constantly as it broke and reformed. A tall, skinny girl in a powder-blue suit broke into the circle between Shevi and me. Shevi kept dancing. I smiled encouragingly at her. A girl with long, blond hair pushed into the circle then and grabbed hold of the tall, skinny girl, knocking Shevi aside without a glance. I was stunned. How could she do that?

Shevi rejoined the circle, winking at me. She gave her hand to a young girl with freckles, whose eyeglasses kept slipping down her nose. A minute later, the freckle-faced girl deserted Shevy and broke into the circle elsewhere, saying in a loud voice, "I just couldn't dance with her!" as if Shevi were blind and deaf.

"Shhh," the woman next to her said. "That's not nice."

"Don't be silly, she's just a midget," freckle-face said.

The more things change, as the saying goes, the more they remain the same.

CHAPTER THIRTY-TWO

REACHING FOR THE TOP

える える

The noise would have been unbearable inside the building. Fortunately they gathered outside; the courtyard of the high school and seminary was carpeted with teenage girls talking at top speed. Most of them were caught up in the excitement of winding up their penultimate year of studies and signing up for their choice of a major for the forthcoming, final year. Tomorrow, the real world would be at their door. Their choice of a field of specialization would most likely determine their whole professional future.

Here and there girls stood in pairs, absorbed in earnest discussion, weighing this important decision.

"What are you going to sign up for?" Ricki asked Penina.

"I'm going to take Elementary Education, with a minor in Bookkeeping just to be on the safe side," Penina informed her.

Shevi stood nearby, taking in the scene. She observed the enthusiasm of her tall friends and kept her thoughts to herself. For them the immediate future held excitement and progress, another rung up on the ladder of their lives. For Shevi it wasn't really a rung to climb, it was the beginning of a new chapter of problems and difficulties the others couldn't imagine.

"Shevi, what about you?" Ricki asked.

"Well, I...I really haven't made a final decision."

"But I thought you wanted to take Preschool Ed," Ricki insisted.

"Well, yes," Shevi hesitated. "But...I don't know...."

"You'd be so good with little kids," Ricki said. "You love children so much." Shevi permitted herself a small smile. Amazing how much power a kind word has to uplift, as much as a cruel one can shatter.

"Don't worry so much, Shevi." Ricki put an arm around her and said sincerely, "You'll be a great success as a kindergarten or nursery school teacher."

Shevi plucked a leaf from a nearby bush and regarded the fresh green color of the tiny bud nestling in her hand. *How helpless it is*, she thought. *How easily it can be torn from its source of life in a fraction of a thoughtless second. Come on, Shevi, your situation isn't that bad*, she chided herself. *Cheer up!*

"*Nu*, Shevi? What about it? What's the problem?"

"To tell you the truth," Shevi confessed, "I'm a bit afraid of the kids themselves." She felt she had to release what was weighing on her heart, even if she'd regret doing so later.

Her friends immediately understood. How would a roomful of young, impressionable little girls or boys treat Shevi? Would they laugh at her? Would they reject her for being different? Ricki and Penina had supported and encouraged Shevi for many years now. They saw beyond the outer, physical covering and appreciated Shevi's remarkable qualities, but they knew that teaching might present some insurmountable obstacles for her. What could they say to this tiny girl with the soul of a giant? Should they cover it over with meaningless chatter and pretend to ignore the problem?

Penina remembered the days when Shevi was hospitalized for one thing or another and lay in bed, pale and weak, connected to so many tubes. She recalled wondering if Shevi would ever have the pink color in her cheeks she so desperately wished for, yet now she stood in the schoolyard just like everyone else, her cheeks glowing with healthy color, thank God.

"Shevi," she began, "I was just thinking about the days when you were so pale and sick and weak, and we all wondered how you would ever overcome all those problems, or if we would ever see you looking as you do now, or if you would ever be able to come to school like everyone else. And now, well...I don't need to bring you a mirror." She smiled happily.

"And you don't need to measure my energy level, either," Shevi answered with a grin. "You're absolutely right! When the obstacles are still in front of us, they seem scary and impossible. What was I thinking of? Of course, it will be hard, it will even be very hard. But with God's help, I'll overcome that too. I'll work very hard and try to be a great teacher so the kids will like me."

Shevi stopped speaking, amazed at her own temerity. Had she really opened up to her friends, here in the schoolyard, just like that? Penina and Ricki were silent, too, but in amazed admiration for their plucky, tiny friend, whose height in inches was minimal, but in spirit and courage towered above them all. Who says, they thought, that a size-eight shoe can make larger strides than a size four?

"...and on Tuesday Shevi will give the demonstration class at the Sanhedria nursery school," Mrs. Weinstein said, "and we'll all observe. Remember, Tuesday at eight o'clock, everyone." Mrs. Weinstein closed her notebook, picked up her briefcase, and left the room. She had been a nursery school teacher herself for twenty years, and now she taught the preschool teachers' training course in the seminary. In the last year of seminary, each student had to give several demonstration classes in her field of specialization.

Uh-oh, Shevi thought. *What am I going to do? How can I stand up in front of all those children and give them a lesson? Maybe they won't even listen to me. Maybe they'll ignore me, or laugh, or get wild.*

The classroom was buzzing as the girls prepared to leave the room, each one commenting on her assignment to give a teaching demonstration at a real nursery school in Jerusalem. They seemed to be competing to see who could come up with the most original ideas. Shevi alone wasn't talking; she was given over to doubts and concern.

In truth, she was not so concerned about the reaction of the children in the nursery school as that of the teacher herself. She had suffered in the past just as much from the scorn of adults as from children's unthinking cruelty; adults also sometimes regarded her as a freak, stared unkindly, assumed she was mentally or physically impaired, and simply had no idea that she was fully cognizant of their attitude. Fortunately, at this point in time Shevi only had to worry about one teacher and one class of children. She could not foresee the obstacles that awaited her after graduation, when she would be looking for a job. She was still cocooned in the warm atmosphere of good and devoted friends who loved her and respected her abilities.

"Shevi, don't worry so much," Shula told her. "You have a real rapport with kids, and you have a nice voice, too, not rough and hoarse like mine."

"Don't exaggerate, Shula. All you have to do is smile at them, and the children will be putty in your hands." Shevi meant the compliment and was sure that her friend Shula would be a great success in her chosen field.

All that week Shevi made outlines and tore them up; she wrote and wrote and wrote: topics, ideas, drawings, and sketches. Maybe she would talk to the children about butterflies — pass out colorful drawings of butterflies and teach them about colors; perhaps she should draw a mouth with a toothy smile and pass out toothbrushes, explain to the children about the importance of brushing their teeth, and use the drawing to demonstrate. She thought of a hundred different ideas, each with its pros and cons, trying to imagine how the little girls would react. She imagined herself standing in front of them, and she felt a tiny stab in her heart. Would they listen to her at all? Would they wonder about this strange-looking student-teacher who was almost as small as they were? As she sat thinking these thoughts, she happened to glance down at her tiny, high-heeled shoes.

Her thoughts turned to her parents. "How lucky I am to have such wonderful parents...they go to so much trouble to have shoes sent from the United States for me, so that I don't have to wear children's shoes, shoes that would make me look ridiculous." She recalled her recent attempts to shop for shoes in Israel, where the only type of shoes the salespeople would show her were more suitable for an eight-year-old than an eighteen-year-old. It was so embarrassing.

Thirty-two pairs of eyes were watching her! Shevi stood in front of the kindergarten class on her own. It was sink or swim. Mrs. Weinstein, the kindergarten teacher, and some of Shevi's classmates were sitting quietly to the rear of the room, and thirty-two little heads were turned expectantly toward the front. Her materials were assembled neatly on the desk next to her and, with a shy smile, she picked up one of the charts she had prepared and began to speak.

"Look at these pictures, children. Hashem has given us all a most important organ — our ears. With our ears we can hear the telephone ring, we can hear a tea kettle whistle, and we can hear someone knocking on the door." As she mentioned each item, she pointed to the appropriate picture on her chart. *Baruch Hashem*, the children were all listening to her and looking intently at her drawings. She gave a few more examples of the gift of hearing and showed them some more of the drawings she had made.

"Now I'm going to pass out picture-cards. Each of you will get a set of mitzvah-cards, and when I play this tape, you are going to hear different sounds connected with different mitzvos. When you hear each sound, you lift up the card that shows that mitzvah, all right?"

The little girls were excited. Shevy passed out the cards she had worked on until late in the night.

The first sound was that of a shofar blowing; the second was that of a man reciting Kiddush; and so on. The girls were thrilled as they identified each mitzvah connected to the ear and gave Shevi their complete attention.

Shevi concluded the lesson with praise for the children's cleverness and thanks for their good behavior. The kindergarten teacher thanked her and came up to the front of the room to take over the class. Shevi heaved a great sigh of relief, collected all her materials, and walked outside. Her friends filed out after her, heaping praise on her performance. Shevi herself was filled with joy. Her demonstration had been a success; she loved every single one of those little girls. She knew instinctively that each child is a world in herself, a wonderful little world that can be planted with knowledge and nourished to fruition with the tender care of a loving teacher. A child will thirstily absorb whatever he is taught.

She had taken the first step fearfully, but now it was behind her. She could now calmly face the rest of the practice-teaching tasks with confidence. "A psalm of thanksgiving," she murmured, "...give thanks to Him, bless His Name.... For Hashem is good, His kindness endures forever...."

The term was over; Mrs. Weinstein was grading each student's notebook to give them final marks in the preschool teachers' training course. "Material missing," she marked in one. "Explanation not detailed enough," she wrote in another. "Poor presentation of subject," in a third.

Shevi's notebook was immaculate, and Mrs. Weinstein reminisced as she marked a large "A" on the cover, for she herself had been Shevi's teacher in kindergarten twelve years before. Even then, she recalled, Shevi had to do everything just right, though it was harder for her than for any of the other students. Her memory carried her back and she saw Shevi in the schoolyard, so tiny and frail, exerting herself to keep up with the others. She had never let anything stop her from learning, from climbing her own personal ladder higher and higher, always reaching for the top.

Mrs. Weinstein looked at the "List of Goals" inscribed on the first page of Shevi's notebook. Her goals were, as always, clear. She prayed that Shevi might attain them.

CHAPTER THIRTY-THREE

A LINKED SALARY

ॐ ॐ

There is no such thing as absolute light or absolute darkness, pure white or pure black. We know daylight and night-time, clear light and hazy light, dawn and twilight, luminosity and gloom. Mostly, however, life is made up of a mixture of the two. A tiny ray of light may brighten our darkest moments, and even our deepest joy is sometimes clouded by a sad memory or event.

Shevy's employment as a nursery school assistant was full of light. She loved the sweet, smiling young children who crowded around her every morning and smiled a happy wel-come. She would gently brush back Esti's tangled curls; she would hug little Devora who was afraid of the fly buzzing on the windowsill and explain that the fly was more afraid of her. Spoiled, pampered Saraleh wanted to keep all the toys for her-self, but Shevi patiently taught her that the other children needed to have a turn, too. Yes, there were many bright mo-ments in Shevi's first job.

Several classes of children attended that nursery school, graded according to age. On the first of each month, when the children had all gone home, the director of the school handed out paychecks. The other women received theirs with a smile or a cheerful comment, but Shevi quickly placed her unopened en-velope in her purse and started to leave.

"Aren't you going to look at your check, Shevi?" Miriam, one of the other assistants, asked.

"Whatever it is, it's linked," Shevi replied.

"Linked to what, the dollar? What are you talking about?"

"My salary is linked to my height, I guess, because it's lower than everyone else's." Shevi quietly left the room.

The other women were dismayed and questioned each other, "Why should Shevi be paid less than the other assistants?"

"She is such a devoted teacher; she is really dedicated to her job, and puts in so much effort and extra time with the children."

"Is there anything we can do?"

They meant well and truly resented the injustice done to Shevi, but there was nothing at all that they could do.

Being a teacher myself, I realized Shevi was not being paid a commensurate salary quite soon after she started working in that nursery school. I had already taken the initiative and called the director personally.

"Mrs. Golden? This is Yehudis Bogatz, Shevi Wittow's sister, speaking."

"Yes, hello. What can I do for you?" she asked pleasantly.

"I want to speak to you about my sister's salary. I think you don't understand her value to your school, how much she is contributing to the care and development of your pupils."

"Well, be that as it may, what is it you want?"

"Do you know how much she loves those kids and what wonderful attention and care she gives them? And do you realize how hard she works at preparing all the teaching aids and classroom displays you are using?"

"So?"

"So I think you are discriminating against her. Her so-called salary does nothing but destroy her confidence in herself. Besides, why shouldn't she be paid the same as the other assistants?"

"See here, Mrs. Bogatz, I don't want to offend you, but I

think you ought to realize that we are doing Shevi a favor by employing her. Your expectations for her are much too high!"

"How can you say that?" I said, trying to stay calm and speak politely. "Shevi does no less than the other assistants. In fact, she probably does more."

"She doesn't wash the floor as well as the others," Mrs. Golden said triumphantly.

I was shocked. Shevi didn't clean the place properly? Mrs. Golden had gone too far. "Listen," I said firmly, "if I was the one working in your school and I didn't clean as well as other assistants, would you give me a linked salary because of that? I'm sure you wouldn't."

There was a moment of silence. "That is how it looks to you," Mrs. Golden finally said coldly.

"Maybe you can speak to Shevi's teacher from seminary, Mrs. Weinstein," I begged. "If Shevi were taller, she would be qualified to be a preschool teacher. There's no reason to discriminate against her. She is talented and perfectly suited for the job."

"*If* she were taller," was Mrs. Golden's icy answer.

This incredible incident wounded our whole family, though of course I never mentioned the conversation to Shevi. Nevertheless, Shevi continued to work there as a nursery school assistant and did her best not to let the director's attitude influence her care of and caring for the children.

One day a new child enrolled in the nursery school. The children were seated at their little tables waiting for Shevi to pass out the ten o'clock snacks. The child's mother carried her in and seated her on the one empty chair, said a few words to Shoshana, the teacher, and left. Shevi was handing out the morning snacks when Shoshana called her over to explain the situation. She had spoken to the mother on the telephone the previous evening, and she had accepted Zahava Cohen only conditionally because there was a problem — Zahavale was two and a half, but she couldn't walk. Mrs. Cohen was desperate to find a nursery school that would accept her, and out of the kindness of her heart, Shoshana had agreed to try. However, she had told the woman that the school definitely would not agree to carrying Zahavale outside to play every day, and Mrs. Cohen had accepted that condition.

"Shoshana!" Shevi said, aghast. "I'll carry her outside every day; I'll take it on myself to take her out to the sandbox with the others. How can you even think of making her stay indoors when every other child is outside?" Shevi continued to hand out snacks to the chldren.

Zahavale came to nursery school every day thereafter, and every day Shevi carried the grateful child outside to play in the sandbox with the other children. Her blue eyes shone with happiness and her laughter was music to Shevi's ears.

One day when Mrs. Cohen came to pick up Zahava to take her home, Shoshana told her she was giving all the children notes about a trip to the zoo the next day.

"Don't worry," Mrs. Cohen said, "I'll keep her home tomorrow and I won't even tell her about it so she won't feel bad."

"No way," Shevi said to the two women, overcoming her natural reticence and speaking commandingly. "I absolutely won't let you keep her home. You bring her with her stroller and I, personally, will take the responsibility."

Mrs. Cohen was very moved. She realized Shevi was speaking from her heart and she knew she could rely on her to take good care of Zahavale. "I can't thank you enough," she said, her eyes filled with tears.

What would Mrs. Cohen have said had she known about the clouds that shadowed Shevi's great pleasure in her work?

CHAPTER THIRTY-FOUR

A WEDDING

જાજા

*B*uilding number two resounded with excited cries, happy voices, the sound of doors opening and closing. Women hurried back and forth carrying food and dishes and flowers. The fragrance of baking wafted through the halls. All the lights were on in the Wittow apartment and it was the center of all the commotion.

Ricki knocked at the door and came in carrying a platter of delicious-looking little cakes, all arranged in silver-foil baking cases. "*Mazal tov!* It's so exciting that Shevi's getting engaged tonight," she said.

Bashi took the platter from her and placed it on a side table. "Thanks, Ricki. I know. We're all so happy. Shevi's getting a wonderful young man — a real Torah scholar."

Shevi was engaged to be married! Sunbeams danced in every corner; buds of thanksgiving blossomed in every heart. Our entire world was in bloom.

"Getting ready for my wedding has been the most beautiful time in my life." Shevi sighed contentedly. "I don't think there's a clothing store in Jerusalem we haven't visited," she said with a laugh.

Mommy laughed, too. "I can't even remember what we saw and where we saw it."

We were all sitting in the living room, having a family conference: Esther, Tovah Leah, Bashi, and I, Shevi's married sisters, had joined Shevi, Mommy, and Abba to help make wedding plans.

"Before we can order the invitations, we have to reserve a hall," Esther said. She was the family "executive-director," in charge of arrangements. She pulled a notebook out of her purse and flipped pages until she found what she wanted. "I made a list of prices of the different halls and I marked down what's included in the price, how many people each hall can hold, where the *chuppah* is placed, and so on."

"I've got a great idea," Shevi exclaimed with a huge grin. "Let's reserve Independence Park! Then all the children who want to can come and see the 'miniature bride.' "

We had always been proud of Shevi's ability to make light of her disability and even joke about it, and so we laughed with her.

"If we sell tickets, we can maybe make enough money to buy a luxury apartment," she continued.

"Why not a house?" Mommy added.

"Maybe we should write on the invitations, 'Please don't bring children,' " Shevi suggested playfully, but with an underlying hint of wishful thinking.

"That's an idea. It would be a most unique invitation," Mommy said.

We were so accustomed to using humor to scatter the gray clouds of insult and distress that it had become a family habit. Nevertheless we dearly wished we could somehow convey to as many people as possible an awareness of how easy it is to hurt other people's feelings, how a little thought and consideration for others would alleviate so much suffering.

Shevi sat on a throne of white, surrounded by flowers. She held a scrap of paper in her hand and her head was bent in prayer. She was praying for each and every petitioner who had asked her to remember him at the sacred hour of her matrimony. She referred to the list often, lest she unintentionally overlook a name.

The hall was slowly filling with friends and relatives, doctors and nurses and former hospital acquaintances. When the band started to play the familiar wedding melody and her groom, Tzvika, and his male relatives approached her throne, Shevi looked up with tears of happiness in her eyes. She prayed now that Hashem Yisbarach hear her prayers for all her petitioners and for herself and her husband, and that He cause His Presence to rest upon their new home, which would be built on foundations of Torah.

The setting sun cast its ruby rays across the skies and tinted the clouds with the most beautiful pastel hues. It provided a softly-lit backdrop to the gold-fringed canopy and the motionless tableau beneath it. The tiny, veiled figure in white, looking like a princess, had completed the seven circuits around the groom and was standing with him in the center. She listened intently to every word pronounced.

"Harei at mekudeshes li — You are hereby consecrated to me...."

Everyone in attendance felt uplifted by the poignant emotion of those moments. Everyone joined in the prayer to the Creator of the world that He complete this edifice and that sounds of gladness fill their home, their sanctuary....

CHAPTER THIRTY-FIVE

OBLIGATIONS

ॐ ॐ

"*I* love to visit Aunt Shevi!" said six-year-old Miriam.

"Me, too," parroted four-year-old Pinchas.

"What a nice surprise!" Shevi greeted us at the door of her new apartment with a beaming smile. "What a pretty dress, Miriam, and what a nice *kippah*, Pinchas."

Shevi invited us to sit down on her comfortable new sofa while she hurried to bring us refreshments from the refrigerator. She handed out popsicles, which she always kept in the freezer for her nieces and nephews, and poured cold drinks for us.

"Don't go to so much trouble, Shevi," we told her.

"It's a pleasure," she said. Shevi loved to have us visit as much as we all enjoyed visiting her. "And I love it when you bring the children. Wait till they see the chocolate cake I baked." She proceeded to uncover and slice a luscious-looking, freshly baked cake.

How easy it is to make Shevi happy, I thought. The children were devouring the cake and talking to Shevi in quick, enthusiastic bursts. Bashi and I watched them as we ate our slices of cake.

"Let's all go downstairs and let the children play in the park." Bashi's voice broke into my thoughts.

"That's a good idea," Shevi said, looking affectionately at the children. "But first I want to daven *minchah*."

"It's only three o'clock," Bashi said in surprise. "Sunset isn't until seven-fifteen. You'll have plenty of time later."

"You're right," Shevi said, "but please, don't be angry, I can't leave the house without davening *minchah*. If I go out, I won't be able to relax. Go ahead, I'll be right down."

Two-year-old Yaakov was banging on the table with a spoon; Nechami and Adina were eyeing the pretty flowers in the fragile vase and approaching dangerously close.

"We'll go on ahead," I said, "before the kids turn your house upside down." We started to shepherd the children out the door.

"Why isn't Aunt Shevi coming, too?" they asked.

"I'll be along soon; I want to daven first," she said firmly. She opened her siddur and began to pray, oblivious to the rumpus going on around her. We gave up trying to persuade her.

Shevi had once promised herself to be strong and filter the evil inclination out of her system as scrupulously as she could. To the evil inclination that says, "There's always time to do a mitzvah; you can postpone it and do it later," Shevi's answer was always, "Run to perform even a minor mitzvah...."

Shevi was now working as an archivist in Maaleh Adumim. A new world had opened up to her, a world of manuscripts and dusty tomes, of silent rows of files and packed bookshelves.

She traveled back and forth daily on the winding highway between Maaleh Adumim and Jerusalem. Her fellow passengers in the minibus were less than delighted with traveling, but Shevi, as always, found the good in everything. She praised the view or the smooth ride, or the enjoyable companionship of the women who traveled with her.

One of the women, Daisy, was of a more contemplative turn of mind than the rest. When Shevi spoke so positively about the traveling, Daisy thought to herself, *I really ought to be more like Shevi. What's the good of complaining all the time?*

"Just look at the traffic jam," sighed Meirav. "We'll be stuck for ages!"

"I hate this," Lila exclaimed.

"Why do you let yourself get angry?" Shevi asked her softly. "You should try to imagine we're on a vacation trip, only the drive is lasting a bit longer than usual." When Shevi smiled, her whole face lit up.

"But the air conditioning isn't working!" Lila protested.

"Well, just look what a beautiful sunset it's going to be," Shevi answered. "Uh-oh," she added as she looked at her watch. "I have to get off the bus. Driver, please let me off now."

"What for?" the driver asked.

"I want to daven *minchah* now." In Israel, just about everybody, religious or not, understands such a request. The driver pulled over to the side and let Shevi get off the bus.

The sunset was indeed a masterpiece. Well, it had been painted by a Master Artist, hadn't it? Shevi took her siddur out of her purse and started to pray.

A strong wind was blowing and she had to hold the siddur with both hands so the pages wouldn't turn. She thought to herself, *You see? The wind is like an agent of the evil inclination, trying to give me another excuse not to pray.* She stood there with unconquerable determination and finished her prayers.

Shevi would accept neither traffic jams nor hurricanes as a valid excuse to postpone her obligations.

"Shevi, where will you be for Shabbos?" I asked my newly married little sister. We were doing our grocery shopping together, for Shevi hated going to stores alone.

"We're going to be with my in-laws," she replied.

"Is it hard for you being with your mother-in-law, and isn't the trip tiring?"

"Hard? Tiring? You don't know my mother-in-law!" she replied with a huge grin. "She is just wonderful; she makes everyone around her feel good. She even asks my advice about a lot of things." She paused for a moment, as though searching for the right way to describe her mother-in-law. "You know, she is one of the rare individuals who do not measure me by my height!"

I looked at my sister in admiration. She knew instinctively and immediately who saw her tiny stature and didn't look beyond it. *Thank God*, I thought, *she has been blessed with a noncritical mother-in-law.* To be accurate, Shevi had married into a most distinguished Jerusalem family; her mother-in-law was a veteran educator, a sagacious woman of great insight. Shevi's sisters-in-law were all bright and accomplished. One and all, they welcomed Shevi into their family as a sister.

Shevi and her husband Tzvika were at home. I was visiting with my children. Tzvika was immersed in study, a large *sefer* in front of him, oblivious of the tumult and activity of his nieces and nephews playing around him. A knock sounded at the door; Tzvika's brother burst in.

"Tzvika, please come with me right away." He added in a whisper, "Mother doesn't feel so good."

"Bye, Shevi," Tzvika called out as the door closed behind the two brothers.

I gathered the children together and prepared to take them home. Shevi was white as a sheet, but said goodbye to the children quietly. On the way downstairs, I met one of her brothers-in-law on his way up.

"I'm sorry to tell you this," he said with tears in his eyes. "I'm on the way up to tell Shevi that our mother passed away."

Tears choked us both and not another word was said. How could it be? A woman of only fifty-four! I sent the children home (we lived nearby) and returned to Shevi's apartment to help impart the tragic news. We tried to comfort Shevi; she had been extremely close to Mrs. Gura and was in a state of shock.

The next day we heard that it had happened suddenly, on Shabbos morning. The family was all in shul except for Tzvi's sister Sari and her two-month-old baby. Hatzalah was called, and an ambulance came, but although help arrived within minutes and the medics attempted to revive her, nothing could be done.

Her family and friends felt that the whole world trembled, the world was bereft: Mrs. Gura, of blessed memory, was no more. She had been a mother, not only to her family, but to countless solitary individuals in need of whatever it was she gave them. Shevi's sorrow was deep, painful; she mourned the woman who had been so warm and loving, the woman who had such great love for and understanding of others.

This is the tribute to Mrs. Yehudis Gura, of blessed memory, written by her daughter-in-law Shevi.

> Words from the heart,
> A heart filled with pain:
> A few small episodes
> That may help explain
> How dear was this woman,
> All others, above.
> A true mother to me,
> With caring and love.
> How she accepted me
> Right from the start,
> A friend, not a stranger,
> She took me to her heart.
>
> She could not understand,
> Found it hard to believe
> That there are those
> Who let appearances deceive;
> Those who forget that health is from Hashem,
> Who look down on others
> Much shorter than them.

"Shalom!" she said, "what guests!"
Thus we were welcomed by Mother.
"How long has it been
Since we've seen one another?"
On Fridays, the day is short
And the work is long,
But Ima Gura made us welcome,
We felt we belong.
She served us with drinks,
Sometimes hot, sometimes cold;
She asked about my family, the young and the old.
She asked about my job with real interest, not fake,
And smiled as she sliced us more chocolate cake.

On Shabbos when everyone napped, she came to me.
In her soft, sweet voice she'd ask with sincerity,
Perhaps I would like a book to read,
Or maybe there was something else I need?
And on *motzaei Shabbos* she'd always say,
"Come on, let's help Tzvi and Shevi;
Their suitcase looks awfully heavy."
She always would go that extra mile,
And never, never without a smile.
Oh, I could not finish her praises if I wrote until dawn,
Our tears will not end for our mother...who has gone.

Shevi truly missed her mother-in-law. Ironically, not much
time passed before Shevi herself was taken to the hospital for the
last time. She told me only the week before that she had taken
out the photograph album of her wedding and had spent many
hours looking at pictures of her mother-in-law. Little did she
guess that she would soon see her again in that world where all is
good, that World where the great souls dwell.

CHAPTER THIRTY-SIX

TODAY, NOT TOMORROW

એ એ

*P*urim was approaching. Shevi and I were out shopping. A chill wind blew and the branches of the trees thrashed about. Shevi's legs were aching; walking had become difficult for her, and getting on the bus was a complicated operation.

"I really don't feel well, Yehudis, and I don't know what to get for Mommy."

"Mommy will understand if you just get her a box of candy or something like that," I said. "She knows it's hard for you this year."

"No, no," Shevi answered, her green eyes flashing a message to me. "For a mother you buy something special!"

Shevi was determined to obey the commandment to honor your parents to the maximum. She always had, no matter how hard it had been for her.

We waited for the bus. Not many people notice that some buses are constructed with a luggage compartment beneath them, and therefore to board the bus, passengers have to climb steep steps, built high off the ground. Other buses do not have that compartment and the steps are closer to the ground and consequently much easier to climb. Shevi always preferred to wait for one of the latter type of buses so she could get on unaided. She didn't want anyone's help, nor did she want to endure the looks of commiseration from people who watched her try to climb up on a bus with high steps. I, of course, waited with her.

Several buses passed by, but they were the wrong kind. It was getting colder, too. Finally, the right kind of bus stopped for us and we boarded. It troubled me how much Shevi had to suffer because of little, unimportant things, things that other people take completely for granted, like the height of bus steps.

Shevi was now working at the main office of an organization called Yad Sarah, located in the Bayit Vegan neighborhood of Jerusalem. Yad Sarah is a nonprofit organization that provides expensive medical equipment like wheelchairs, hospital beds, and orthopedic aids, free of charge to those who need it.

Shevi sat down at the computer in her new office. *How lucky I am*, she thought as she turned on the computer. The computer never laughed at her or called her names! *And such nice people here.* Her coworkers, mostly volunteers, treated her with respect and understanding. She felt the urge to give thanks to the Creator of the universe: "Who is like You among the heavenly powers, Hashem?..."

Shevi was then holding down two jobs; in the mornings she worked at Yad Sarah and in the afternoons she worked in a kindergarten for disabled children. She had grown to love the children in the short time she had worked there, and each day as she rode the bus down from Bayit Vegan she looked forward to seeing them.

On the way to the kindergarten, however, she had to pass a girls' elementary school and she dreaded the days when the girls were just coming out of school as she passed by. "Just let me get there before school is out," she prayed. Some days she was successful and reached her kindergarten peacefully and relieved. Some days she had to run the gamut of stares, laughter, and unkind comments.

"Shevi! Shevi's here!" Two little ones ran up and hugged her.

"Shevi, sit down and have something to eat first," her

coteacher said to her. "I'll bet you haven't eaten anything since breakfast."

"I really hate to waste time eating," Shevi answered. "Time is so valuable, it's a shame to spend it eating."

Better than a book of *mussar* was our Shevi, was she not?

The seasons succeeded each other in turn. Shevi was busy and, for the most part, content. Winter had receded, and spring was apparently here to stay for a while. Pesach preparations were in evidence all around. Women had mattresses and rugs airing on balconies; discarded toys, broken dishes, and old suitcases were piled high next to trash bins; and young girls were out walking with their younger siblings in tow.

Shevi sat at a low table in the kindergarten busily rubbing and scrubbing the toys; cheerful music played from a tape recorder.

"You never take a break," her coteacher remarked. "You don't stop working for a minute."

"Well, it has to be done," Shevi replied.

"Not all today, though. We have three more days until Pesach vacation."

Shevi would not let herself be tempted. Three more days — no, she must do today whatever could be done and not leave it for tomorrow. That was her motto in life. *It's not good to postpone things,* she thought. *A person never knows what will happen tomorrow.* So she thought, as her hands busily completed task after task. She was in pain, but she tried to ignore it as well as she could.

Shevi didn't know it, but that was to be her last day in kindergarten. That very night, the tragic closing chapter of her life was to begin.

CHAPTER THIRTY-SEVEN

A HOME FAR AWAY

଼ଈ ଼ଈ

I slowly open my eyes and glance at the clock — seven in the morning. The apartment is still quiet and peaceful. The birds chirp cheerily in the trees and I think I'll enjoy another few minutes in bed before getting up to wake the children and set the day's activities in motion.

The phone rings.

"Good morning," I say.

"Yehudis...." Shevi's voice. "Excuse me for phoning so early," she whispers.

"What's the matter, Shevi?" I cry out in alarm.

"I...I've been up for hours, Yehudis. I...I'm having trouble breathing....I don't know...."

"I'll be right there!" I say.

"Oh, thank you...so much!" She sounds relieved.

Shevi's apartment is quite near mine, and I am able to get there quickly. I pass some men hurrying to morning prayers. I can hardly breathe, I am so frightened.

Shevi's husband Tzvi opens the door for me and I rush into the bedroom. Shevy is lying in bed, gasping for breath. One of her hands is terribly swollen and she can't move it. "Shevi!" I cry. She tries to smile. I help her to sit up and prop her up on pillows.

"Thank you...Yehudis," she whispers. "I feel awful...to bother you...and it's just before Pesach."

"A real bother, indeed," I say. I help her to sip a glass of tea her husband has brought in for her. She breathes a bit easier.

"Look, I'm going home to get the children ready for school," I apologized, "but I'll be back in about half an hour, *b'ezras Hashem.*"

I hardly notice what I am doing. I go home, do what I have to do, explain things to my husband, call my mother, and then I'm sitting at Shevi's side once more.

"Yehudis, I really...feel...terrible...to have you waste...valuable time...on me...and just when...you have...so much to do...at home," Shevi manages to say, pausing in pain after every few words.

My heart is pounding and I can hardly see straight. My hands tremble as I wrap her robe around her, and Tzvi and I half-carry her down to wait for the taxi. "Thank you...so much...Yehudis," she says.

Mommy pulls up in a taxi and we get Shevi settled inside; they drive off. I stand there with Shevi's words ringing in my ears. "Thank you!" Thank me? Shevi is incredible. No one else reaches anywhere near her height in *middos.*

Shevi is in the Hadassah Hospital Intensive Care Unit — big, black letters spell it out on the door. White-garbed nurses hurry to and fro. Black and white, life and death: hospital colors, hospital atmosphere.

Shevi, too, is in white; white sheets, white face. She is attached to a myriad of tubes and machines, which beep and blink in the background. Only one person at a time can visit a patient in this room; the rest of the family members must sit outside in the corridor on benches or in the waiting room down the hall.

Bashi approaches the guard. "May I go in?"

"Patient's name? Your relationship?"

Bashi tells him. He picks up his phone and speaks to someone inside.

"All right. You may go in, but just for ten minutes."

Bashi's heart thumps loudly; she is so anxious to see her beloved twin.

"Bashi," Shevi smiles at her sister. "How...wonderful of you...to come."

Bashi is distressed to see her sister so weak and in such pain, but it is so good just to be with her.

"Why don't you...bring over a chair?" Shevi asks; as usual she is worrying about someone else.

"If I bring a chair in here, they'll throw me out," Bashi jokes.

"Poor you! I'm so...glad you came. How is...everyone? How are...your children?" She is truly interested, never mind the tubes in her arm, never mind the swollen hand, the pains, her weakness....

"I'm sorry," says a sympathetic nurse to Bashi. "You have to leave now. But you can come back in an hour."

Shevi worries what Bashi will do for an hour. "You don't have to wait," she reassures Bashi.

Take note, Bashi thinks, *how it is possible to forget the self and think of others. Shevi is always showing us how we can improve ourselves.*

Shevi was tossing in pain. She was no longer in intensive care, but her hand was still swollen and bandaged, and she was still hooked up to several machines. Night was about to drop its dark hood over the world and she might have seen the first few stars winking in the cold, steel-gray sky, had she been able to look out the window. It was probably the last cold spell before the winter gave way once more to spring, and it was the first night of Pesach.

The moment she caught sight of her twin sister Bashi coming through the door, she forced herself to lie quietly and tried to smile.

"Bashi. How nice that you can be with me tonight. What a

pretty dress...wear it in good health." Bashi was dressed for the holiday.

"I brought something for you, Shevi," said Bashi, holding up a small package.

"Please open it for me," Shevi said weakly.

"Oh, that is so cute." Bashi had found her a mug with a small mirror inset. Inscribed on it in gilt letters were the words: "Smile, life is beautiful."

"Whenever a sourpuss nurse comes over, you can show her this," said Bashi with a grin. Shevi grinned back.

"I'm so sorry you have given up your seder to be with me. You could be home with your husband and children, enjoying yourself...." Shevi tried to detect a trace of disappointment in her sister's face, but all she saw was a pleased, warm, loving smile.

"I love to be with you, Shevi. You know that."

"Well, I appreciate your...sacrifice, anyway." Shevi murmured.

Into the dark shadows of the hospital, Bashi was able to bring a small but powerful light. All around lay patients confined to their beds, too ill to go home for the holiday, dependent upon harried nurses busily rushing to and fro. All eyes turned to the two young women, to the two tiny candle flames shimmering on the bedside table, to the pretty matching cups and plates Bashi had set out: a real seder table.

Mrs. Brim, a congenial woman in her fifties, smiled from the neighboring bed and listened contentedly as Bashi started to read from the Haggadah.

"*Kadeish*," Bashi intoned. Then, "*Urechatz....*"

Bashi conducted a perfect seder, pronouncing each blessing with deep emotion. The other women in the room added their voices when Bashi softly sang the traditional melodies: *Avadim Hayinu, Betzeis Yisrael, Echad Mi Yodeia, Adir Hu.* Finally, "Next year, in a rebuilt Jerusalem — in good health!" They all answered with a fervent "Amen."

"That was the most beautiful seder I've ever seen!" said Mrs. Brim.

Two tiny candle flames had banished the darkness and flashed a ray of hope to everyone in that room.

Bashi cleared away the remains of the feast and retired to a small cot the nurses had set up for her. The candles flickered out, and they all slept.

Shevi lay there thinking of her family: her dear husband, her parents, her sisters and their growing families. Oh, how she missed her twin's children. Bashi's adorable three-year-old had just had his hair cut. Her six-year-old was going into first grade the following year and Shevi had asked to buy her her first school bag. Why had Bashi looked at her so strangely? How Shevi yearned to see her in her new school uniform.

"Hi, Shevi!" Her cousins Shmuel and Nili came in. "How was seder night? How did you manage? Who asked the Four Questions?"

"You know I'm...the smallest...so I...did the asking." They laughed together, momentarily pushing off the knowledge of where they were and why they were there.

Her guests sat with her for a long time, sincerely enjoying her company. Shevi, as usual, remembered to ask about each member of their family, even though it was a great effort for her to speak.

"You know, Nili," Shevi said at one point, "I have a dream...of moving closer to my mother. We don't live...that far away from each other now, but...soon I'd like...us to look for...another apartment."

"It's good to live close to one's mother if you can," Nili agreed. "I heard your mother is looking for an apartment for you on the same block."

"Still...I have a funny feeling...that I'll never...live close.... I'll be...living...far away...from Mommy...."

Nili and Shmuel were shocked into silence. Soon they said goodbye to Shevi and left — with a terrible feeling of foreboding.

A few days later, Mommy and I were in a cab riding home from the hospital. It was midnight, and the cellular telephone rang.

"Shevi's being taken down to intensive care!" Tovah Leah told us.

The moment we arrived home, we alerted Abba, Esther, and Bashi, and soon the five of us were in Abba's car heading back to the hospital. With tears in our eyes, we said *Tehillim* all the way.

Tovah Leah met us outside the intensive care unit.

"What happened?"

"I don't know. She suddenly felt bad, I called the nurse, and they brought her here immediately." Tovah Leah was pale with shock.

An hour later, a doctor emerged from the unit and informed us that Shevi was in critical condition. We clutched our *Tehillim*s tightly and prayed as hard as we could.

At dawn, Abba decided that we must conserve our strength and marshal our forces. Just Mommy and I stayed in the hospital; the others went home. At six o'clock, the doctors permitted us to go inside and see Shevi.

She was able to talk, though obviously she was very weak. "Have you...been waiting...long?"

"Shevi, how do you feel?" We smiled fondly at this little sister who worried about us while she herself was critically ill.

The nurses came by regularly to check all the monitoring machines; the staff was alert and very attentive.

"How...is Tovah Leah? She...was with me for...so many hours."

"Is the pain very bad?" I asked.

"Pain? Oh, you know.... Right now...I'm fine...with you

and...Mommy here." Her eyes shone with love and gratitude. We stayed with her for a little while, then went outside and waited. Eventually — I can't remember an exact sequence of events — Mommy and I went home for a while when Tzvi, my sisters, and Abba replaced us, taking turns at keeping vigil.

At some point, the nurses told us that Shevi had gone into a coma, and they brought in a respirator.

"May I see her?" Mommy asked with a racing heart.

"You can go in, but you must understand she is attached to a respirator."

Mommy entered the intensive care room slowly and stood next to Shevi's bed. "Shevi, my Shevi," she whispered. "Mommy's here with you. Don't worry, with God's help it will be all right." Tears of suffering welled up from her soul. She prayed the prayer of a devoted mother watching over a beloved child.

Mommy pulled over a chair and sat next to the bed. She whispered soothing words, reassuring words to her daughter to reduce any aura of anxiety that might penetrate Shevi's subconscious. Her heart overflowed with love as she watched her daughter's sleeping face. She began to hum an old lullaby she had sung when the twins were infants: *"Lulei Torascha sha'ashuei* — Had not Your Torah been my delight, I would have perished in my affliction." Then: *"Ani ma'amin b'emunah sheleimah* — I believe with perfect faith...."

Surely Shevi could hear her; surely she could sense that her mother would never leave her side. The monitor showed a rise in her blood pressure when Mommy sang to her.

All her family members stayed near, each of us racked with sharp, burning pain. Had we shown Shevi enough love? Had we been aware at all times that she was a precious gift from the Creator? I watched Mommy as she unflaggingly sang one song after another to Shevi in her sweet, melodious voice, songs from *Tehillim*, songs of thanksgiving, songs from her heart. They were songs she had sung to us through the years, and I remembered each and every one of them. Scenes from our childhood appeared to me: happy, shining hours; hours spent laughing and playing together as young children; hours of sharing so many good things as we grew up; and of course, ever present, the unforgettable hours of dialysis we shared with Shevi.

In all those scenes, one common thread ran through both the good times and the more difficult times — our shared feeling of *simchah*, of happiness at being together.

CHAPTER THIRTY-EIGHT

HIS NAME IN ISRAEL IS CONSOLATION

ઢ ઢ

*E*sther was making a bris milah for her newborn infant. When our car pulled up in front of my parents' house, right next to Abba's car, Abba called over to me, "I'm glad you're here. You have a phone call, Yehudis." He handed me his cellular phone.

"Yehudis, please come back to the hospital right away." Shevi's sister-in-law Shira had stayed in the hospital so we could all go to the bris. A member of the family always stayed with Shevi; though each of us left her physically from time to time, our hearts and minds were on constant watch.

"Come back?" I burst out crying. "What's happened?"

"Her breathing suddenly got worse. It sounded so heavy and...and I think you should come back."

"Did the doctors tell you to call us?"

"Not exactly...I think you should come right back." Shira's voice was shaking.

Abba and I looked at each other in confusion. He had heard my side of the conversation, but — we were all dressed up and ready to go to a bris milah. He had been waiting for Mommy and Moishy to come downstairs. What should we do?

"Shira," I said hoarsely, "maybe you could ask the doctors? Maybe we could just stop by for a few minutes at the bris and then come?"

"Yehudis...." Her voice was strange. "Don't you...understand?"

"What, Shira? What are you trying to say?"

Shira was weeping now. "Yehudis...she's...gone...."

I screamed the awful words into the phone. "She's gone? Shevi's dead?"

Abba burst into tears. "She-e-e-evi! My daughter! It can't be!"

"We'll come right away," I sobbed to Shira and closed the phone.

"*Baruch Dayan HaEmes!*" Our neighbor and dear friend Rebbetzin Ruchoma Shain was standing there on the sidewalk with us. "You'll go to the bris!" she commanded us. "And you're not telling your mother, do you hear me?"

"But Shevi is gone!" Abba said in anguish.

"Listen to me! You must go to the bris, and not a word to your mother." We were in such total confusion, we could never have decided on our own. We felt we had to listen to Rebbetzin Shain's clear voice of command and do as she said.

Mommy came out of the building then, dressed up for the bris, but we could see she had been crying. A moment earlier she, too, had been talking on the telephone. She had called Esther and had said to her, "Esther, please listen to me now. I want you to call the baby 'Refael' because it means 'the Almighty heals.' I want Shevi to be remembered Above...."

Esther had agreed immediately, with tears pouring down her cheeks.

Just when Mommy had been saying, "Refael, may Shevi be remembered forever," Shevi had returned her soul to God.

We went to the bris. We felt as though we were in a whirlpool and were being dragged down and down. Abba went over to speak to Esther's husband.

"Esther." Her husband went over to her. "Please give the baby to the *kvaterin* for a moment, I have to talk to you." Bashi took the infant from her arms.

"Esther, try to stay calm. The baby will not be called 'Refael,' but 'Menachem' [one who consoles]...and your mother doesn't know yet."

"*Oy! Ribbono shel Olam!*" Esther understood, and grief overwhelmed her. She struggled to maintain her composure, but everyone was crying anyway, thinking of Shevi so far away in the hospital. Bashi handed the baby to the *sandek*, who cradled him on his knees. Everyone was thinking of Shevi, only most of those present did not realize that Shevi was even farther away than they knew.

The baby was called Menachem. Mommy looked questioningly at Esther. Tovah Leah also wondered why.

"Mommy," I whispered in her ear, "we won't stay for the meal; Shevi's condition is critical...."

Rebbetzin Shain came over to us, bless her. She put her arm around Mommy and said quietly, "Listen to me now and try not to be too upset. It's for her good, for Shevi...."

Mommy knew. "No! Shevi, my Shevi, you haven't left me all alone. You, who always worried about me." Her sobs and laments rent the air.

Even the heavens wept. Large raindrops fell to earth, and it seemed to us that the whole universe must be mourning the loss of our Shevi.

At the moment when her soul ascended, her family was dressed in festive clothes, attending a *simchah*. At the hour when the angels escorted her pure soul to its heavenly abode, we were welcoming a son, grandson, and nephew to the Covenant of Abraham. A half-hour after Shevi's passing, a "healing" was granted to her family. His name in Israel is Menachem.

Shevi, dear daughter and sister, pray for us! Pray for your devoted husband, for your loving father and mother, for your adoring sisters and brother, and for all the House of Israel, pray that Hashem grant each that which is lacking. Now you are near to the Lord of all the worlds. Please plead for us!

Tributes to Batsheva, ז״ל

י שלום ירושלים

לשון - יום שני ד' אב תשנ״ח

יעקב, פת, קטמון, רמות א' וב' ושמואל הנבי

נושא השנה - ״נשיאה בעול״

האולם הכחול נתרם לע״נ האשה מרת בת שבע גורא ע״ה
בת יבלחט״א הרב אסא ויטו שליט״א
The Blue Hall is dedicated in memory of our very special and beloved
Bas Sheva Wittow Gura ע״ה
who always looked forward to participating in the inspiring evening
of Shmiras Haloshon.

In Memoriam

Fortunate is he who lives with a good name
And leaves this world with a good name.
What do people say of him?
"Fortunate is he, who lived with a good name
And dealt in Torah and mitzvos
And in good deeds all his days,
And was righteous, pious, and God-fearing,
Who loved the One above,
Who loved mankind,
Who loved righteousness,
Who loved uprightness!"
And since others testify thus of him,
The Holy One, Blessed be He, welcomes him,
Forgiving all his sins.
For thus have our Sages, of blessed memory, taught,
"Which person is destined for the World to Come?
As it is written: And your ears will hear
What your brothers speak, saying...."

The Virtues of Good Qualities, Virtue Fifteen

Dedication from Abba

The Chafetz Chaim, *zt"l*, used to tell a parable from which much can be learned:

A peasant owed a nobleman forty thousand rubles. The time came when the debt was to be paid, but the peasant had managed to scrape together only half the sum, only twenty thousand rubles.

The angry nobleman punished him severely with twenty strokes of the lash.

When the king heard of this, he was furious, saying, "What good does lashing do?" Turning to the peasant, he said, "You have now been found worthy to take possession of half of the nobleman's house, which is equivalent in value to twenty thousand rubles!"

To the king's astonishment, the peasant burst into tears.

"What is the matter?" asked the king.

"It is too bad I wasn't given forty strokes of the lash," the peasant explained, "for then I would have earned the whole house!"

Indeed, if we were on the proper spiritual level, we would

ask Hashem for a large portion of suffering so that we would earn a larger portion in the World to Come. Suffering purifies; it readies us for eternal life.

When my daughter Shevi, of blessed memory, underwent her first transplant operation, rejection took place after only four days! How well she knew the pain and suffering of a transplant operation. Despite this, when she was taken into the operating room for another transplant, she said with a smile: "Wonderful! Thank God! I am going to have another transplant!" and her face glowed with joy. Shevi knew that, despite all the suffering, after pain comes rest, comes soothing.

Until she was four years old Shevi could not walk. I was full of doubts about how Shevi would grow up. Could she ever be happy? Would there ever be a time in the future when she would smile? Yet, in spite of all the pain, a smile lit her face always. Her bright smile gave us, her parents, the strength to cope in all situations — it was a smile that lit up the hearts of all those around her.

During the mourning week, we heard a stream of stories, stories about the heroism of my daughter, my little Shevi. Most of the stories we had known about; we had lived with them in her lifetime. Even as a young child Shevi was special. We, her family, sensed that we had in our possession a living *"mussar sefer."*

Heartbroken, I cannot believe that she is no more....

I turn to you, Shevi, now that you have gone on to that world which you readied for yourself in your lifetime: Be a righteous advocate for your mother, who cared for you always, for your devoted sisters, your dear brother, for all of us, your bereaved family!

Your Abba

Batsheva: A Mother's Story

*B*atsheva taught me how to live. How to live in this world with suffering and pain, and how — alongside it, together with it — to have a lot of *simchah*, great joy.

Shevi appreciated everything anyone gave her — a cassette, a barrette — every piece of her clothing reminds me of her "thank you." Anytime I took her anywhere — which for me was the greatest pleasure — she gave me her *todah rabbah*, her "thank you for taking me, thank you for coming with me." Thank you, thank you, were Shevi's most often repeated words.

When we were in America years ago, after a hospital stay, I took her out shopping — it gave me such happiness to see her in new clothes. After a few days, she told me, "No more clothes for me. Now you, Mommy, you'd better buy something for yourself." I reassured her, "Don't worry, when I find something suitable, I'll get it." Well, we went into a large store. I looked around for something for myself. I couldn't find anything I really liked, but suddenly I saw a lovely blouse which was perfect for Shevi. I told her, "I'm not asking you, I'm buying it!"

When we walked out of the store, on the sidewalk of that busy street, I saw there were actually tears rolling down Shevi's cheeks. "What did I do to you, Shevi?" I asked in concern.

"You didn't buy anything for yourself," she cried. "Why did you buy for me?"

She always worried about me. On Chol HaMoed Pesach, a

Wednesday morning, the doctors told me to call the whole family to come to the hospital. Her condition was most critical, and it was unlikely she would last much longer. The end was near. We were all there, crying and davening. As I prepared myself to say goodbye to Shevi, I thought, *How terrible! It's the month of Nissan; there will be no hespedim, no eulogies for Shevi. How can that be? I can't bear that.*

Well, Shevi must have been listening, in her coma in the next room. She must have told *HaKadosh Baruch Hu,* "My mommy wants me to have *hespedim.*" And she stayed with us another month, until Iyar, so she could have the eulogies I so much wanted her to have.

We had an extra three weeks with her — so we could pray, say *Tehillim,* do *teshuvah,* think about who she was, and say goodbye.

It was never hard to take care of Batsheva. She had such *simchah,* such joy and appreciation for everything life had to offer. She was so easy to love. No complaints — never did she let me know how much pain she suffered. She didn't want me to worry or to feel bad. I had to guess and understand to know what she didn't want me to know.

She went to work every day. Even on that Tuesday when she fell so critically ill, she worked a full day — eight in the morning to three-thirty in the afternoon. She came home, cleaned a closet for Pesach....without a word to anyone — not to me, not to her husband, not to her sisters — about how bad she felt.

That night, when the fever and infection and terrible pains began, her husband took care of her through the night. She would not let him call me. "We have an appointment tomorrow morning at the clinic anyway," she said. "Let's pretend you're not taking care of a sick wife, let's make believe we have a new baby and we have to be up at night to take care of him."

Her whole life was "Let's pretend. Let's pretend I have no pain...."

When Shevi worked in a nursery school years ago, the toddlers loved her. The children who knew her loved her; those who didn't know her, children on the street, hurt her. They stared at her. They were cruel to her.

During the mourning week, the grandmother of one of those children in the nursery school where she worked for five years came to me and told us the story about the child who couldn't yet walk at the age of two and a half because of a heart condition. The grandmother told me they had agreed to allow the child to be left inside when the others went out to play because who would pick up a two-and-a-half-year-old every day and carry her to the sandbox?

Shevi would. She wasn't going to let that child suffer from loneliness, for she herself knew only too well about loneliness, about being different, about being stared at.

Shevi never let herself be pitied. She went out into the world and did what she had to do. She studied hard; she worked hard. She enjoyed life as much as she could and would not let her physical pain stop her. She would not let the world's cruel stares, cruel indifference, and cold pity ruin her life.

Yes, whoever knew Shevi loved her. Those who didn't know her were cruel to her, but she rose above it; she ignored it and lived her life with joy. Shevi was a lesson to me. She taught me how to live, how to look at all the joy in life, the great beauty in the world, and to ignore the pain, the suffering, the loneliness. She had a lot to teach the world.

On one of the last days before she fell into a coma, she told a visiting niece of mine, "My mother is looking for a different apartment for me to move into. There's one in her building, but it's too expensive. I know she wants me to live near her, but somehow I have a feeling I'm going to live far away from my mother."

Batsheva, you are special. We didn't know just who you are. People say you had the funeral of a *gadol*. You are a *gadol*.

Shevi, you took care of me all your life. You helped me. You taught me how to live. I hope you will continue to take care of me and to pray for me. And for all your family. And to help bring the Mashiach.

May she rest in peace

From Batsheva's Husband, Rabbi Tzvi Gura, שליט״א

What was the key to the success of my dear wife, Batsheva, of blessed memory, through which she succeeded in being so good — and so universally beloved? It was her lack of egotism. She always thought about the other person, how she could help others, how she might succeed in bringing about some good for another person.

Even at her job in nursery school, where she was so successful, she didn't work solely for the money, but rather, she always thought of how she could improve the situation for others.

Rav Chaim Friedlander, *zt"l*, in his booklet, *Shalom BeAhalecha*, writes: " 'If you will lend money to My people...' (*Shemos* 22:24). Rashi says that you should see yourself as if you were a poor man. Because as long as you don't feel yourself to be poor, you can't bring benefit to the poor man as you should."

So Shevi was: she always thought of the other person, as if she were in his place. Therefore, she understood how the other person felt.

Though things were difficult for her, she always rejoiced in another person's happiness, and from this root-source all her virtue flowed. As Rav Dessler, *zt"l*, writes in *Michtav MeEliyahu*, part I, "The quality of giving causes the person to become good, and vice versa, Heaven forbid, the quality of taking is the root of evil that causes all evils."

Shevi had the root of giving; she was always giving to everyone. How can we give her something back? What was it that she wanted from us? It hurt Shevi that children looked upon her as someone different and unfortunate. It hurt her that they stared or laughed at her — didn't they know this caused pain?

"Why do they think that we, the small people, are blind or deaf?" she would ask, painfully, when people said hurtful things near her. It hurt her very much that parents would see their children laughing and not stop them, not explain to them that it's forbidden to laugh at others. Because if a child laughs and the parents say nothing, or worse, if they laugh with him, why shouldn't the child keep laughing?

It is necessary and important to explain to a child that it is forbidden to laugh at others and to what extent that laughter can hurt. If this isn't stopped, the child becomes accustomed to laughing at others and later it will be difficult to stop him. As the Chafetz Chaim writes about *lashon hara*, "If children are not taught not to speak *lashon hara* when they are young, it is hard to stop them later."

Shevi wanted this book to be written, since the subject of laughing at people and making fun of them caused her so much pain in her life. If that goal is achieved, if this book helps put a stop to such insensitivity — it will be toward the ascent of her soul.

I thank my father, may he live and be well, for his help and support all along the way.

I thank my wife's parents, may they live and be well, who were always solicitous of our needs, from the major down to the most minor detail, and were with us all along the way.

A special thank you to all those who helped and assisted in the publication of this book, in the merit of my dear wife, Batsheva, of blessed memory, especially her dear sister Yehudis, who wrote it.

May Hashem grant that no further loss or destruction be known within our borders. And with the consolation of Zion and Jerusalem, may we be consoled.

Amen.

From a Neighbor

A MEMORIAL TO THOSE WHO ARE GONE

Upon the conclusion of the week of mourning for Batsheva Gura, a"h

Perhaps it was the cold that gripped us all from the inside, and perhaps, for your sake, Shevi, the heavy heat wave broke. We stood outside, all of us, hundreds if not thousands of people, and parted with you.

We parted. Sounds strange to put it that way; grating to the ear and wrenching to the heart. Could it be? That I would never meet you again, going on a Shabbos stroll with your nieces and nephews? That I would no longer encounter your pleasant face when you came to exchange books in the library? That I would never again have the pleasure of your warm "hello"?

I stood together with the others and heard what was being said about you, and icy chills crept up my spine until they reached my heart — and shattered together with it. They emerged externally in the form of teardrops, slivers and fragments of a broken heart. I wept and everyone around me wept. We cried and I will continue to do so for a long time.

You were twenty-seven years old when you were taken from

us. In Hebrew letters, it is "*zach*" years, and as the word denotes, you were *zach*, pure. Your body was pure and your soul was pure.

Batsheva, you were like a seven-year-old in that you achieved the true perfection of innocence. You reached the maximum of your potential. Even in unbearable situations, you did not backslide, but held your own and became all the stronger. You took giant steps toward perfection — and you reached the goal, the finish line.

You could not possibly have done better; you could not possibly have been purer, as Rav Ezrachi testified: "A soul clean and righteous." At twenty-seven, like seven, in beauty. Batsheva, you were like your name: you had the pristine, innocent charm of a seven-year-old. You weren't like other women in their twenties, concerned only about enhancing their looks. Rather, you were like Sarah Imeinu, who related to her beauty like a seven-year-old.

You retained your natural innocence, and the inconsequential vanities that never interested you in childhood did not tug at your heart later on, either. Batsheva, you were like a wholesome seven-year-old, and that's how you will always remain for me.

Pray for me, Batsheva, plead and pray for me, that the foundations that were laid in my heart will endure forever, that I will continue to learn from you, to draw something from the totality of your virtues, the vast range of your merits, and that the lessons deeply etched within me remain forever.

Rest in peace; you have reached your goal. Now you can reap the reward you so richly deserve.

BATSHEVA WITTOW GURA MOURNED IN JERUSALEM

By Mattis Goldberg, IJN

Correspondent in Jerusalem

During a week which displayed an intense Jerusalem heat wave, God suddenly poured forth tears of rain as more than one thousand Jerusalemites accompanied Batsheva Gura to her final resting place.

Shevi, as she was known to all, was the daughter of native Denverite Asa Wittow, who has lived in Jerusalem for thirty years, and the granddaughter of Mrs. Milton Wittow of Denver.

Shevi was born with kidney problems and suffered greatly during her twenty-seven years of life, yet she always had a smile on her face.

Over one thousand people came to console the Wittows during the week of shivah, including many yeshivah heads and rabbis and two former Knesset members.

Rabbi Yitzchak Ezrachi of the Mir Yeshivah eulogized Shevi, quoting two verses from The Song of Songs:

"The watchmen that go about the city found me, they smote me, they wounded me; the keepers of the walls took away my mantle from me. I adjure you, O daughters of Jerusalem, if you find my beloved, what will you tell him? That I am love-sick" (*Shir HaShirim* 5:7–8).

Rabbi Ezrachi explained that although Shevi was sick for much of her life, she accepted all of her suffering with love.

He said that Shevi was always happy, especially when it came to someone else's happy occasions. Shevi was more concerned about others than about herself.

Her father, Rabbi Asa Wittow, a frequent visitor to Denver, spoke about Shevi's love for every Jew. "Whether it was a Jew from Russia, Denver, or Jerusalem, Shevi loved them all equally."

Rabbi Wittow said that when Shevi was a year old, he had to travel to England. Since he was going anyway, he asked a doctor if he should bring Shevi along for tests. The doctor told him that it wasn't necessary. Rabbi Wittow later found out that [according to her medical records] the doctor didn't think Shevi would live out the year. Instead, she lived an extra twenty-six years, a gift from God.

Rabbi Wittow was in tears as he described his wife's dedication to Shevi all her life.

The principal at the high school Shevi attended said that he does not remember one time when he saw Shevi without a smile on her face.

One charity collector, who came to the Wittow home every week, was shocked to hear about Shevi's death. The collector never realized that anything was wrong with Shevi because every time she came Shevi always greeted her with a warm smile.

Shevi didn't grow fully and had a hard time walking. One family member revealed that the looks of pity she received brought her more pain than the physical suffering she endured.

She always hoped that people would learn to act properly to all people they meet, including those who appear different. Indeed, people who knew Shevi well treated her with complete respect because they understood that they were in the presence of a very special person.

Shevi's mother, Hannah Wittow, emphasized how Shevi knew how to live life with *simchah* (happiness). Although she suffered, she had a special love for life.

Shevi's younger brother, Moshe Wittow, spoke about how careful Shevi was to treat every person with respect. She made sure to honor everyone, including people younger than she.

A week before Shevi passed away, tens of thousands of Jews worldwide who study the *Daf Yomi* (daily Talmud page), studied *Shabbos* 153.

The Talmud says that people are not moved to tears when they hear about the death of an acquaintance. Therefore, people are asked to eulogize the deceased in order to elicit a feeling of sadness in the hearts of people, and bring forth tears from their eyes. However, as emotional as the eulogizer might be, people will respond with tears only if the deceased was a righteous person.

During Shevi's funeral, as the eulogizers were recalling her life, many people were crying — genuine tears were flowing from their eyes. From the scene of the funeral, it was obvious to us all that Batsheva Wittow Gura was a righteous person.

BATSHEVA GURA, a"h
by Yated Ne'eman Staff

Special to Yated Ne'eman

26 Iyar, 5758 (May 22, 1998)

Hundreds of people participated in the *levayah* of Batsheva Gura, *a"h*, which took place on Thursday, the eleventh of Iyar.

Batsheva was born in 5731, twenty-seven years ago, to her parents, Asa and Hannah Wittow, who came to Eretz Yisrael after their wedding to establish their home upon a pure Torah foundation, amidst exceptional *mesiras nefesh*, leaving family behind. This home was, in fact, exceptional in its open and hearty hospitality. Week in and week out, their Shabbos table was filled with dozens of young people of various backgrounds, all of whom Reb Asa and his wife successfully were *mekarev* and many of whose *shidduchim* they made and who now have produced second generation homes of Torah and *chesed*.

It was in this vibrant atmosphere that Batsheva grew up, and its joyful holiness permeated her entire being. Reb Asa was a staunch adherent of his mentor, HaRav Chaim Pinchus Scheinberg, *rosh yeshivas* Torah Ohr, and would not make a move, great or small, without consulting his *da'as Torah*. In addition, he was *meshamesh* the Rosh Yeshivah in countless ways, primarily by transporting him to and from yeshivah, a privilege he would not relinquish to anyone else! This subservience to a *gadol baTorah* is markedly reflected in the home where Batsheva grew up.

Batsheva herself lived a life of physical suffering, which was not always evident from the outside, because she took her handicap in stride. Always pleasant-mannered, sweet, and happy, she was beloved by all who knew her, young and old alike. Batsheva married a *ben Torah*, Reb Tzvi Gura, son of Reb Moshe Chaim Gura, and established a true home of Torah and *yiras Hashem*, a model of a fine Jewish home. Throughout her married life, she stood firmly by her husband's side and encouraged him to the best of her ability in his dedication to Torah.

The hundreds of mourners who attended the funeral heard *hespedim* from her family whom they have held in high regard for the past three decades. First of the *maspidim* was Rav Chaim Dovid Altusky, *rosh mesivta* in Yeshivas Torah Ohr, who called upon the public to arouse themselves to increased levels in view of the fact that the deceased had so purified herself in her mere twenty-seven years (the numerical value of "*zach*") of her lifetime.

Rav Yitzchok Ezrachi, a *rosh yeshivah* of Yeshivas Mir, stressed the attribute of *simchah*, which had been a hallmark of the deceased, a fact that was most unusual considering her physical difficulties. Not only that, he said, but she was also able to genuinely share the joy of others.

Rav Yaakov Bornstein movingly described the house in which she had imbibed all her wonderful traits, of which *simchah* was outstanding.

Rav Yisroel Ganz, a *rosh yeshivah* of Yeshivas Kol Torah, dwelled on the verse in *Shir HaShirim* which tells that Hashem went to the garden to pluck roses. Why does He pluck roses? Because the garden is overrun with thorns and they cannot grow. Batsheva, he said, had reached pure and exalted levels in her years of *zach*, twenty-seven, and did not fit the garden.

Reb Moshe Weinberg, a brother-in-law, wept aloud and said, "The walls of the *ezras nashim* in Yeshivas Torah Ohr will cry out this Rosh HaShanah: 'Where is Batsheva? Where is the woman who always came to pray even when it was so difficult for her?' "

The deceased's father, Reb Asa, wept that his daughter had never wanted to cause other people unnecessary trouble. On the very night before she went to the hospital, hardly able to breathe, she refused to wake anyone up, but waited until morning. She was a living lesson of loving one's fellow man. May she be a good interceder for all those who were so devoted to her.

Her brother, Moshe, noted that the body is referred to as *kavod*. It is our mission to elevate the body to the spiritual level of the soul. Batsheva was outstanding in the trait of showing respect toward others, even young children, with whom she worked, and her young nephews and nieces. He begged *mechilah* for her *kavod* in the name of the entire family.

Another brother-in-law, Reb Mordechai Bogatz, quoted the Chafetz Chaim, who says that in the times preceding Mashiach, the individual's suffering would serve as atonement for the *Klal*. Through her unwavering *avodas Hashem* amidst personal hardship and suffering, Batsheva aroused us all to grow closer to Hashem.

Batsheva was buried on Har HaMenuchos, accompanied by the throngs that prayed that she be a *melitzas yosher* for her people.

YN

Photographs

GLOSSARY OF HEBREW TERMS

Abba — Father, Daddy

Acharei Mos — one of the weekly Torah readings

Adar — Jewish month in which Purim falls

afikoman — the portion of matzah broken off to eat at the end of the seder

a"h — may she/he rest in peace

avodas Hashem — service of God

baruch Dayan HaEmes — blessed is the True Judge (traditionally said when one hears of a death)

baruch Hashem — thank God

bas — daughter of

bedikas chametz — search for leavened bread the night before Pesach

ben Torah — Torah scholar

berachah — blessing

b'ezras Hashem — with the help of God

bitachon — trust in God

bris milah — circumcision

bruchah haba'ah — welcome

chametz — leavened bread, not eaten on Pesach

chametzdik — containing *chametz* or having had contact with *chametz*

charoses — mixture of nuts, fruit, and wine eaten at the seder

chasan — bridegroom

cheder — a religious boys' school

chein — charm

chesed — kind-heartedness; giving to others

Chol HaMoed — the intermediate days of Pesach and Sukkos holidays

Chumash — Five Books of Moses

chuppah — wedding canopy; wedding ceremony

chutzpah — effrontery

da'as Torah — Torah view

daven — pray

Emor — one of the weekly Torah readings

erev — the day or evening before

ezras nashim — women's section

gadol — a great person

gadol baTorah — a person great in Torah learning

Haggadah — prayer book containing the service recited at the Pesach seder

halachah — Jewish law

hamotzi — blessing over bread

Hashem — the name of God

Hatzalah — first-aid emergency organization

hechsher — rabbinic approval on food

hesped (pl. *hespedim*) — eulogy

Ima — Mother, Mommy

imaleh — help! (slang term)

kallah — bride

kavod — honor

Kedoshim — one of the weekly Torah readings

Kiddush — blessing said over wine on the Sabbath and holidays

kippah — skullcap, yarmulke

klal — the community

klal Yisrael — all the Jewish people

Kosel — the Western Wall

kvaterin — couple honored in the circumcision ceremony

lashon hara — gossip, slander

lechem mishneh — two pieces of bread which begin a Sabbath meal

levayah — funeral

madrichah — counselor

Mah Nishtanah — four questions recited at the Pesach seder

Mashiach — the Messiah

maspidim — eulogizers

matzah — unleavened bread

mazal tov — congratulations

mechilah — forgiveness

megillah — a sacred scroll

mein tochter'l — my little daughter

mesiras nefesh — self-sacrifice

middos — character traits, especially good ones

minchah — afternoon prayers

minyan — quorum of ten men

mishloach manos — packages of food exchanged on Purim

mitzvah — a commandment

Mordechai HaYehudi — Mordechai the Jew

motzaei — conclusion of

mussar — Jewish ethical teachings

mussar sefer — book of ethical teaching

pesachdik — used for Pesach

Purim — a holiday celebrated in the Jewish month of Adar

Purim gelt — a monetary gift customarily rewarded to the messengers who deliver Puriim packages

rav — rabbi

rebbetzin — rabbi's wife

refuah sheleimah — complete recovery

Ribbono shel Olam — Lord of the Universe

Rosh Chodesh — first day of a new month

rosh mesivta — instructor in a yeshivah

rosh yeshivah — head of a yeshivah

sandek — man honored with holding the baby during circumcision

Savta — Grandmother, Grandma

sefer — book

segulah — merit

Sephardim — descendants of Jews who lived in Spain or Portugal

seudah shelishis — third Shabbos meal

Shabbos — the Sabbath

shemiras halashon — guarding one's tongue

Shemos — Exodus

Shir HaShirim — the Song of Songs

shlita — may he live many years

shloshim — period of thirty days after a death

shofar — ram's horn

siddur — prayer book

simchah — joy; a happy event

tefillos — prayers

Tehillim — psalms; the Book of Psalms

tenaim — betrothal

tochter 'l — little daughter

yasher koach — good for you; thank you

yiras Hashem — fear of God

Yisbarach — Blessed be He

zach — pure

zechus — merit

z"l — of blessed memory

zt"l — of blessed memory (used for a righteous person)